AMAZING STORIES

EDMONTON OILERS

D1092144

EDMONTON OILERS

Stories from the City of Champions

HOCKEY

by Rich Mole

PUBLISHED BY ALTITUDE PUBLISHING CANADA LTD.
1500 Railway Avenue, Canmore, Alberta T1W 1P6
www.altitudepublishing.com
1-800-957-6888

Extreme care has been taken to ensure that all information presented in
this book is accurate and up to date. Neither the author nor the
publisher can be held responsible for any errors.

Publisher	Stephen Hutchings
Associate Publisher	Kara Turner
Series Editor	Jill Foran
Editor	Megan Lappi

We acknowledge the financial support of the Government
of Canada through the Book Publishing Industry Development
Program (BPIDP) for our publishing activities.

Altitude GreenTree Program
Altitude Publishing will plant twice as many trees as were used
in the manufacturing of this product.

We acknowledge the support of the Canada Council for the Arts which
in 2003 invested $21.7 million in writing and publishing throughout Canada.

Canada Council   Conseil des Arts
for the Arts   du Canada

National Library of Canada Cataloguing in Publication Data

Mole, Rich, 1946-
Edmonton Oilers / Rich Mole.

(Amazing stories)
Includes bibliographical references.
ISBN 1-55153-798-2

1. Edmonton Oilers (Hockey team)--History.
I. Title. II. Series: Amazing stories (Canmore, Alta.)

GV848.E36M64 2004   796.962'64'09712334   C2004-903749-8

An application for the trademark for Amazing Stories™
has been made and the registered trademark is pending.

Printed and bound in Canada by Friesens
2 4 6 8 9 7 5 3

This book is dedicated to all the hockey entrepreneurs who take the risks and make it happen.

Contents

Prologue

It was 1990. Mark Messier, the captain of the Edmonton Oilers, faced the biggest challenge of his young career. He needed to carry the Edmonton Oilers through the playoffs to the team's fifth Stanley Cup victory without "The Great One" by his side. The Oilers had not been able to do it the year before. Two teams had met to battle for the 1989 Stanley Cup, but the Edmonton Oilers had not been one of them. Messier and the others had consoled themselves with the simple fact that making the finals — and winning them — was no piece of cake in a league of more than 20 teams.

The Oilers' playoff run got off to a rocky start. But after being down 3-1 in their series against the Winnipeg Jets, the Oilers were finally able to turn things around and pull the tough series out of the bag. Then, it was on to round two. Playoff pressure was bad enough. Making it worse, Messier knew that he lived in the shadow of the team's former captain and "spark plug" Wayne Gretzky. But he also knew that his team wasn't just good — they were great. Now it was time to prove it.

Messier pulled on his skates, laced them tight, and got ready to meet his former captain, Wayne Gretzky, and the L.A. Kings. It was game one, round two, of the 1990 Stanley Cup playoffs.

Chapter 1
New Team in
a New League

he biggest news story in National Hockey League (NHL) history was announced with a one-word headline — EXPANSION. In September 1967, after years of uneasy speculation and stone-walling from profit-conscious team owners, the NHL doubled its size, transforming itself from a 6-team eastern league to a 12-team league that embraced cities on both coasts and as far south as St. Louis, Missouri.

Edmonton: A Hurtin' Hockey Town

Lost in the excitement of new expansion teams in cities such as Philadelphia, Pittsburgh, and Los Angeles was the *other* story — the story of disappointment and disillusionment in Winnipeg, Cleveland, and Edmonton. In the years that immediately followed, these cities found themselves shunned by the suddenly expansion-shy NHL. All of them argued they should be big-league towns. Nowhere believed that as fervently as Edmonton, because once upon a time, the city had been a big-league town with its own professional hockey team.

Supported by the Detroit Red Wings, the Western Hockey League's Edmonton Flyers had given the city a fabulous 10-year hockey run, starting with their first championship season in 1952-53. Those had been wonderful years for a President's Cup winning team of great players bound for NHL careers. The roster had included future big league stars such as Al Arbour, Norm Ullman, Johnny Bucyk, and goalie Glenn Hall. Flyers coach Bud Poile, a former Stanley Cup winning Maple Leaf, suggested that the Western Hockey League (WHL) form a western division of the NHL. Perhaps the WHL could form a second big league to compete with the NHL.

However, when Poile left Edmonton to coach the San Francisco Seals, he took Edmonton's dreams of big-league glory with him. The Flyers went into a tailspin and failed to make the Western Hockey League playoffs. Unimpressed, Detroit withdrew its support and Edmonton was forced to drop out of the league. Calgary was forced to do the same. Any hopes WHL backers had of becoming a part of the NHL or forming a rival league were dashed when the now-tiny WHL folded. Any dreams Edmonton had of being part of the only existing professional league died, too. Edmonton was a hurtin' hockey town.

When Edmonton hurt, William "Wild Bill" Hunter hurt. As the force behind Edmonton's Junior A team, the Oil Kings, Bill Hunter wanted the big league more than most. Hockey had been in the redhead's life since his father had managed a team in Saskatoon. When Hunter made the transition from a North Battleford sporting goods store operator to a Regina hockey team owner, it seemed a natural progression. Then he moved to Edmonton.

Hunter had backed the Oil Kings after their 1962 Memorial Cup victory. Within three years, the Oil Kings won the Cup again. While Hunter took great pride in the performance of his Oil Kings — seven consecutive runs at the Memorial Cup was extraordinary — there was always the feeling of what could have been, what *should* have been.

One day, Hunter received a call from Walt Marlow, a former Edmonton hockey nut who was now a sports reporter for the *L.A. Herald Examiner*. Marlow was home to visit his father and wondered if Hunter had a few minutes to spare. When Marlow and Hunter met, Marlow got straight to the point: he wanted to know what Hunter thought about the new hockey league that had just been formed. Even though he was co-owner of one of the most successful Junior A hockey teams in Western Canada, Hunter hadn't yet heard about the World Hockey Association (WHA). It didn't take long for the Oil Kings co-owner to see the possibilities. It took him even less time to start promoting it, with the kind of evangelical passion that had become the Wild Bill trademark.

Before long, Marlow had introduced Hunter to the men behind the WHA: Gary Davidson and Dennis Murphy. The two Californians instantly recognized Hunter's significance. This was a man who not only knew the game inside out, but also knew those who owned and managed the teams. He knew exactly who had the money it took to turn hockey dreams into reality. Hunter also owned a winning team (and the team's arena), in one of the cities shut out by the NHL. Davidson and Murphy couldn't believe their good fortune, and neither could Bill Hunter. Maybe the hurtin' was over.

Edmonton Momentum

Wild Bill Hunter was not only happy to lead the attack on the NHL, he was absolutely delirious about it. His frontline offensive was right there, in Edmonton. His battle tactic — a reorganization of the Oil Kings. The first order of business was to change the name of his team from the Oil Kings to the Alberta Oilers; the second was an injection of new players.

"Major league hockey at its best," Hunter's press release thundered, but then added, "any player who talks to me about placing the money for a three-year contract in the bank before he signs won't be talking to me ten minutes later." Hunter targeted former Flyers and members of his Memorial Cup winning Oil Kings, snatching many from NHL rosters, including former Oil Kings captain, Glen Sather.

The third order of business was a new hockey showcase

for the new team. A replacement had to be built for Hunter's small 5800-seat Edmonton Gardens, and fast. "If the city of Edmonton doesn't announce an arena in the next two months, we'll build one ourselves," he said. However, Hunter first needed to build support for the new team. It seemed simple enough. After all, this was a hockey town. All Hunter had to do was exactly what he did best: sell, sell, sell! As he began to build Edmonton momentum, Wild Bill Hunter was also building league momentum.

The term "press conference" hardly conveys the spirited rah-rah atmosphere of the rallies Wild Bill staged during those exciting days and nights. The media had always enjoyed Oil Kings press conferences, but now these loud, boisterous freewheeling media blitzes were newsworthy events in themselves. Bill had plenty of detractors, but he disarmed them. "I welcome criticism. I expect heaps of criticism. Criticism is healthy." He promised that the Alberta Oilers and other WHA teams would leave those "can't-do" naysayers in the dust.

"World Hockey Comes to Town," the new billboards shouted. "Follow the Crowd. Buy Now." Edmonton fans did what they were told. They started buying season tickets. Everyone felt they were buying more than seats in the Edmonton Gardens — they were buying a piece of a dream come true.

No Fun at All
Wild Bill Hunter's make-it-happen optimism notwithstanding,

nothing worthwhile is accomplished easily. In its early days, the World Hockey Association proved that particular rule over and over again. During the initial 1972-73 season, the WHA's Philadelphia Blazers made a big announcement: the Blazers would take on the NHL's Philadelphia Flyers. There was a little hitch, however. The Blazers' rink staff hadn't quite got the hang of making ice. Every time the players skated on the rink, the ice cracked. The game was called off.

In Edmonton, the ice was great, but the team playing on it wasn't. Hunter fired his coach and took on the job himself, but the Oilers finished out of the playoffs. Nevertheless, Edmonton — and all other 11 teams in the league — had actually completed their first season, which was more than many NHL honchos (and perhaps a few WHA owners) had expected.

As the 1974-75 season began, Bill Hunter watched as construction neared completion on the new Northlands Coliseum, the hockey showcase he had championed. That year, Edmonton made the playoffs, although they were quickly eliminated by the Minnesota Flying Saints, four games to one.

The following season, Hunter managed to lure a big-name veteran from the NHL, goalie Jacques Plante, although Plante failed to meet the expectations of the fans or the coach. A 3.32 goals-against-average was one reason for the team's less than inspiring 36-38-4 performance. Bill Hunter soon went back to work on the team's roster.

By the next year, hockey had become more work than fun for WHA operators. Some players returned to the NHL and losses mounted. A few months before, Team Canada, made up of WHA players, had lost a series to the Soviets. A losing image was not what the league needed at this tense time. Then, suddenly, WHA teams in Vancouver, Toronto, and Phoenix all disappeared in a sea of red ink.

Oilers owner Bill Hunter wasn't having much fun, either. Four different coaches — including himself — in four seasons hadn't made any difference to the success of the team. In spite of having the highest average attendance in the league (over 10,000), the team was still losing money. Wild Bill figured it was time to sell. The buyer was the Edmonton General Hospital's former chief of surgery and trust company owner, Dr. Charles Allard — an early Edmonton WHA backer.

It didn't take the good doctor long to realize he didn't like the team's losses or the public criticism that resulted. He liked the financial strain even less. A fast-moving, B.C. millionaire named Nelson Skalbania had been putting big-scale real estate deals through the Allard family trust company. When the doctor asked him if he would be interested in purchasing a hockey team, he said yes.

Share the Wealth, Share the Debt
The first thing a new WHA owner usually does after he buys a hockey team is formally announce that he's done the deal. Nelson Skalbania decided there would be a slight change

in priorities. After he examined the team, its books, and its prospects (the Oilers had finished the season a dismal fourth in the five-team Canadian division), the West Coast entrepreneur realized it could be *years* before he saw a profit from the team. So, "quick-buck" Skalbania decided that the first thing he had to do was unload at least part of his hockey team. The questions was, to whom? The answer came quickly: his friend, Peter Pocklington.

The man he chose to share the potential wealth and the present debt — close to $3 million of it — was a fellow millionaire who had started selling cars while he was still a teenager in London, Ontario. Pocklington left classes at age 17 ("I was fired from school," he said) so he could concentrate on selling. Somewhere on the road to success he decided what he really wanted was to be wealthy. So that's what he set out to be, using the cash from car sales to do it. Peter Pocklington was the salesman's salesman. Running his first Ford dealership while barely in his mid-20s, he moved four times as many cars off the lot as his predecessor. A second, larger dealership soon followed. Then, Pocklington asked Ford to look for an even bigger one for him to buy. In 1971, Ford found one in Edmonton. Peter Pocklington moved west, at just about the time Wild Bill Hunter was revving up Edmonton's WHA engine.

As decisive as he was upon occasion (he signed the deal on the Edmonton dealership in about half an hour), Pocklington took the long view, nurturing along various investments for years, including real-estate properties in the American Sunbelt. Soon, he was acquiring and nurturing financial services and natural resource interests, as well.

When Skalbania asked him if he would be interested in buying a piece of Edmonton's WHA franchise, Pocklington agreed to talk. It was then that Nelson Skalbania held his unorthodox news conference.

One fateful evening in October 1976, as Peter and his wife Eva were enjoying dinner at the Steak Loft restaurant, the doors opened and Skalbania arrived with a gaggle of reporters in his wake. The bartering began.

When it was over, Pocklington's vintage 1928 Rolls Royce, two of his valuable oil paintings (both men were art collectors), and a mortgage note for $500,000 worth of real estate changed hands, along with a stunning ring that Eva slipped off her finger. "Worth at least a hundred thou—" Pocklington assured Skalbania. In return, Pocklington received 40 percent interest in the money-losing team and shouldered half the debt. Both men were happy with the deal.

Now that Pocklington and Skalbania were partners in hockey, the talk turned to the future. How long would it be before the Oilers could retire the debt? How long would it be before they could turn a profit? The question was not just how long, but simply *how*. Both men agreed on the answer to that question: when the letters "WHA" were replaced with the letters "NHL." It couldn't happen fast enough to suit Skalbania. That was too bad, as it was bound to be a long-term proposition — the kind he hated.

In spite of the long-term gamble that hockey teams represented, Skalbania had developed an itch that he just couldn't scratch. By 1981, he had bought a total of eight hockey teams, including Calgary's. One of the teams was a franchise in Indianapolis called the Racers. Like many other WHA teams, the Indianapolis Racers needed a lot of help. Gate receipts were lousy. That was no surprise — who wanted to pay to see a loser? Even some people who knew what Skalbania had paid for the team (one dollar, plus the debt) wondered about his decision.

The long-term problem, of course, was how to get the NHL to take in these teams. In the meantime, Skalbania desperately needed to find a way to get people to come and see his teams play. Maybe, just maybe, there was one solution to both problems. He needed a star attraction to interest both the fans and the NHL.

Chapter 2
The Kids

ayne Gretzky was very upset. He called his dad from Sault Ste. Marie, where he was wearing number 99 for the Soo Greyhounds. He phoned home often to pour out his frustrations. His father, Walter, urged patience, although Wayne didn't have much patience left.

Sault Ste. Marie was a long way from Brantford, where Wayne Gretzky had lived with his family, had gone to school, and had tried (and failed) to live the life of an ordinary teenager. He had been out of the house, away from his hometown, his mom, dad, little brothers, and sister for more than two years, since he was 14. That was not a typical experience for a young teenager. Things had not been "typical" back home, either — not for a 10-year-old who could score 378 goals and win a season scoring title by a margin of 238. That was when the pressure, envy, and jealousy had begun. Four years later, Wayne was eager to leave, *had* to leave. Besides, big-time hockey was calling.

His first stop was the Metropolitan Toronto Hockey League's Young Nationals.

In Toronto, Wayne lived with the Cornishes. They were the family of a fellow player, so it was like a home away from home. In another and unpleasant way, life in Toronto felt just like life back in Brantford. Things got, well, difficult. Just trying to play for the "Nats" was a trial — or close to it. The league had a rule: Toronto boys only. So, the Cornishes made Wayne their legal ward. When the league wouldn't budge, they went to court. In the end, the league won the case. Wayne's response was to go back down to Young Nationals Junior Bs, to escape the rule and win rookie-of-the-year award. Yes, it was just like home.

His second stop was the Junior A Greyhounds in Sault Ste. Marie.

When he was drafted to the Greyhounds, Wayne enjoyed another home environment with the family of Steve Bodnar, a friend from his peewee hockey days. The Greyhounds GM Angelo Bumbacco was good to the boys on the team and to Wayne. So was the coach, Muzz McPherson. It was a great season: 70 goals, 112 assists, and trophies as best rookie and most gentlemanly player. Then, things got difficult again. This time it wasn't a problem outside the rink; it was a problem inside the rink.

Coach Muzz McPherson had resigned and Paul Theriault had taken over. Theriault had theories and he wanted changes. One change concerned Wayne's positioning in the play. Theriault wanted Wayne to be exactly wherever the action for the puck was the heaviest. That sounded pretty logical, but Wayne had been playing a different way for years.

Out in the backyard rink, Walter Gretzky had taught his son to skate away to where the puck was going to go, to *anticipate*. That way, when the puck arrived, Wayne would be there, waiting for it. Walter's way worked. Even before he left Brantford, people had been referring to Wayne as "The Great One." Virtually every time he went onto the ice, Wayne demonstrated that the word was more than simply a catchy adjective hung on his name.

Getting Good

For close to 15 years, young would-be, could-be hockey stars would stare up at a Wayne Gretzky likeness thumbtacked to their bedroom walls. They would lie on their beds, maybe after a practice or game, finger the newest Gretzky gum card, and wonder — how do you get that good?

Here's a secret. First, you have to start young.

One afternoon, two-year-old Wayne Gretzky was gazing at the TV, mesmerized by the flash and twirl of the hockey players on the screen and the rising crescendo of the arena crowd. Suddenly, Wayne's grandmother walked into the room and shut off the set. She was stunned when Wayne burst into tears, thinking he was being punished for being bad.

Little Wayne had barely begun to walk, but a few months later, during the winter, he was already on skates. Walter Gretzky, crouching down low behind his movie camera, captured images of his tiny son as he lurched around on the ice, grinning into the lens.

Far away, in the Quebec town of Lachute, at the rink next to Lowe's Dairy, it was the same story. Two or three times a week, the Lowe family would bundle their youngest into his snowsuit, and Clifford Lowe would take him to the rink, help him put on his skates, and then watch as three-year-old Kevin ventured onto the ice all by himself. A couple of years later, Kevin watched his older brother, Kenny, play goal. Kenny was already so good that he and his father sometimes talked about what it took to be a professional. Kevin heard his father say that if Kenny wanted to be a pro, he needed to act like one. Now was the time to start training. Kevin — one day destined to be a star Oilers defenceman — was listening.

Another secret: you have to have the right parents.

Just outside Portland, Oregon, kids would get together near Highway 26 to play hockey on a frozen pond. They always tried to play a little harder, a little faster, when Mark, his older brother Paul, and their dad would come down. The boys, even little Mark, were league players. However, it was Mark's dad, Doug, the boys wanted to impress. Doug was a *real* hockey player. He was helping WHL's Portland Buckaroos get to first place again for the third time. It was funny, though — although Doug would skate around a bit and shout encouragement, he would never actually play with the kids. They said it was because he was afraid he would hurt one of them. He was tough, went at it hard, and got all those penalties. Could he hurt someone? When they saw Mark Messier's dad play, the kids could believe it. Mark, who would one day be an Edmonton Oilers MVP, was already starting to play that way, too. He was only five.

Another famous hockey dad had played Junior B and knew exactly what it took. He didn't have it himself, but he thought maybe his son Wayne did. He was Walter Gretzky, an everyday guy with five kids, a house, a mortgage, and a job at Bell Canada. Later, many found it hard to believe that someone who appeared to be so ordinary could be The Great One's father.

They didn't know about the backyard rink Walter Gretzky had planned and built every winter, with a sprinkler rotating slowly in 20-below weather so the ice would be uniform and smooth. They hadn't been watching as Walter had shaved down the lightest hockey stick he could find to fit his little boy. They hadn't seen him shoot passes in Wayne's direction as the small youngster had hopped over sticks carefully positioned on the ice. They hadn't been there to hear the kind words of encouragement. In those early years, Walter's job, as he saw it, was to help Wayne find out if he had what it took to make it. He wanted to give the kid a chance.

In his book, *Champions*, Kevin Lowe says simply, "everything I learned in hockey since those childhood days goes back to what my father pushed me to do. I owe him a lot ...."

His family's commitment to the game began long before Kevin Lowe was born. By donating the rink's refrigeration plant, Lowe's Dairy had helped make skating and hockey a reality for many kids in Lachute.

A few days after Kevin was born, the Lowes were happy and relieved. It had been a difficult labour, but mom and the new baby boy were just great. Driving home from the hospital, Clifford informed his wife, Jessie, that he wouldn't be home after dinner that night. The rink had scheduled a meeting for that very evening. Clifford said he felt obligated to attend, but he also really wanted to attend. Jessie was put out. She wanted to know if hockey meant more to Clifford than his brand new son. The proud papa thought about it for a moment and then explained that Kevin might want to skate and play hockey someday. By going to the meeting, he would be working for them all.

"Little did I know how involved I would become with hockey," Kevin's mom later confessed.

A third secret: you have to want it more than anything else.

One valuable lesson Kevin, Wayne, Mark, and many other Cup-winning Oilers learned from their parents was one that applies to any goal worth pursuing on or off the ice, and that's commitment. Fortunately, when nothing matters as much as being out there with skates on your feet and a stick in your hand, commitment comes more easily.

Mark Messier and his brother Paul "wanted to play so badly," their sister, Mary-Kay, remembers. "They always wanted to go to practice. They played continuously for hours and hours." In fact, little Mark was barely old enough to be enrolled in elementary school when his lively imagination put him out on the rink, lifting the big, shiny, silver Cup above his head.

Back in Lachute, Clifford Lowe chatted with Kenny about hockey, discussing what the future possibilities were. His younger brother Kevin was listening, too. If Kenny wanted to be a pro, Clifford told him, he would have to eat, drink, and sleep hockey. School was first, followed by church, and then hockey. Little Kevin filed the information away.

However, Kevin quickly learned that some of the tests of his commitment would have nothing to do with what happens on the ice. In Lachute, the Lowes represented the English-speaking minority. Kevin's rapid rise in peewee hockey was rewarded early. He was made team captain. Clifford offered his congratulations and then suggested that with his new leadership role came new responsibility. It meant phoning the kids on the team, boosting their morale, and giving them instructions. It also meant a new, difficult level of commitment. The kids on the team were French-speaking and Kevin didn't speak the language. Although Kevin pleaded with his dad, Clifford was adamant — Kevin would have to learn French.

The next secret: you have to love it.

For Messier, Lowe, Gretzky, and future Oilers teammates Paul Coffey, Glenn Anderson, and Grant Fuhr, the love of the game was so great that anything — school or a part-time job — that kept them away from the rink was regarded as work. Playing hockey was different. Once the pads were buckled on, the skates were laced, and the guys stepped out onto the ice, the hours flew by.

"Nobody told me to practice three hours a day," Wayne Gretzky confided in his autobiography. "I practiced all day because I loved it."

The fourth secret: you have to have ability.

Most young people — and their parents — learn early on that without talent, satisfying achievements probably await off the field, court, diamond, or ice. Playing the game because you enjoy it is simply not enough. At the same time, latent ability must go beyond physical prowess and strength. If all of Wayne Gretzky's abilities were physical, he would have been "The Pretty Good One" instead of "The Great One." His skill and personality made him good. They also made him vulnerable to hockey's formidable bruisers.

"I'm Phyllis Gretzky," Wayne's mom told Bobby Hull in a hotel before one of his early games. "I don't want you hurting Wayne in those corners tonight," she warned him.

If the ability to mete out and endure physical punishment was what the game was all about, then Wayne's future was dim. The superlative athlete, however, had other abilities — mental abilities.

The top achievers on the team — any team — see the game differently than many of their teammates. What seem like isolated moves are perceived by the Messiers, Gretzkys, and Kurris of the world as components of very natural and obvious patterns. These mental abilities don't come naturally to most. It takes time and practice to hone those skills to near-perfection. (Ask any owner who wonders why he spent so much money on a young player who just isn't getting it fast enough!)

For most of us, the mental effort alone would be exhausting. Now couple that with full out, continuous physical exertion. For many players, the passion burns so brightly that there is a willingness to endure the drills and exercises over and over again. It is this conscious effort that makes a crucial difference to physical performance. Mental skills are important, but a dedicated work ethic can compensate for talents far more modest than those of Gretzky or Messier, and can elevate even an average player to moments of greatness.

"Absolutely," Wayne Gretzky told writer Peter Gzowski. "It's all practice. I got it from my dad. Nine out of ten people think it's instinct, and it isn't." When Wayne told Gzowski how hard it was, it was 1981. Wayne's real work, and those of his new teammates, still lay ahead.

The final secret: you have to be willing to pay the price. After a quick pass to the scrawny 10-year-old with the big ears, grim-faced parents took out their stopwatches to see how long it would be before Wayne Gretzky would release the rubber to somebody else, like maybe their own kid for once. It didn't matter that his team — and theirs — eventually won the game. It didn't matter that Wayne racked up 120 assists in 79 games. They had a name for someone like Wayne Gretzky: "Puck Hog." He wasn't the only one they yelled at. Up in the stands, the abuse hurled at Wayne Gretzky's father became so upsetting that his wife wouldn't even sit with him.

Life is full of desires and decisions. Peter Pocklington wanted to be wealthy. He wanted it badly enough that he simply made a decision to be rich. Getting to be an outstanding hockey player is much the same. Lowe, Messier, Gretzky, and many others wanted it so much that they simply made a decision to be the best.

Chapter 3
Gamesmanship

Gus Badali was Wayne's new agent. Gus knew that the NHL didn't take underaged players, but the WHA did. John Bassett, the owner of the Birmingham Bulls, offered Gretzky a one-year, $8000 contract. Badali shook his head. The Whalers offered an eight-year deal with a signing bonus of $200,000. Before Gus could put a pen in Wayne's hand, the Whalers, hoping to make it into the NHL, pulled out at the last moment. There was no use irritating the league because they had signed an underaged 17-year-old, right?

Wayne was becoming desperate. All he could think of was Gus Badali and the offer from the Birmingham Bulls. He phoned home again, begging his father to call Bulls owner John Bassett and get him out of Sault Ste. Marie.

A Foot Race to the WHA

Gus Badali had gotten his first look at Wayne Gretzky a year or so before, while he was playing for the "Junior Nats" in Toronto. Walter Gretzky had first heard about the newly established agent from other players' parents. When he asked Badali if he would be interested in a new client, Badali agreed to add Wayne to his small roster. By 1980, that roster would grow to 40 players, including Edmonton Oilers' first-draft choice, Paul Coffey.

Gus Badali was standing in the lobby of the Hotel Toronto when Nelson Skalbania stepped out of the elevator. Skalbania was there because the WHA was holding a meeting. Badali was there because a good player's agent goes where the deal makers gather and where connections are made. Of course Skalbania had already heard about Wayne Gretzky — who hadn't? His tip on the wonder boy came from none other than John Bassett, the man who had failed to sign him for his own team.

Badali wasn't surprised to see Skalbania at the hotel. The surprise came when Skalbania reached into his inside pocket, gave Gretzky's agent $1,000, and ordered him — well, offered a firm suggestion, anyway — to get the Gretzkys on a plane to Vancouver. Once they got out there, Skalbania implied, they could do a deal.

Skalbania's knowledge of Gretzky was merely by word-of-mouth. He had never watched him play, but for the moment, that was unimportant. He knew that if he had heard good things, the NHL executives had also heard good things. That was enough, right there. Still, a buyer had to have some demonstration of a player's abilities. So, after Nelson Skalbania drove the Gretzkys and Badali out to his palatial house in his Rolls Royce, the fun began.

Wayne smiled and nodded politely, but secretly, he was exhausted. He had not slept the night before and had just endured a four-hour flight in a cramped airplane. Now came the zinger.

"Hey, how about a little run?" asked veteran jogger, Nelson Skalbania.

Seven miles and one steep hill later, Wayne had managed (somehow) to pull away from the older but still physically fit businessman. After the two of them arrived back at the house, Skalbania felt quite confident. Wayne felt like he was at death's door. They all agreed to meet in Skalbania's office a few minutes later.

Now Skalbania had the confirmation he needed. It was obvious that Gretzky had the stamina he was looking for. Based on all reports, he would also be able to provide the kind of crowd-pleasing hockey needed to bolster the Racers' sagging revenues. Wayne Gretzky would definitely be an exciting addition to the Racers, or even to the Houston Aeros, another team Skalbania was thinking of purchasing.

Skalbania's more ambitious objective went far beyond getting a star performer for the Indianapolis Racers. He secretly wondered if that star performer, Mr. Wayne Gretzky, might just be the way to get the Racers into the National Hockey League. He knew that even if the NHL didn't want the team, they might be interested in its star performer. That was the real game. It always had been.

The NHL had already made an agreement with the Canadian Amateur Hockey Association to never entice a player under 20 years of age away from the amateurs. The player-starved WHA ignored the agreement and happily courted the young, hot players sweating it out on junior hockey teams. It was a good way to fill team rosters immediately and a great insurance policy for the future. Developing these young hotshots for three or four years meant the WHA could have a league full of superstars by the early 1980s.

However, the NHL threatened to lobby the federal government about the WHA scooping up all the underaged players. League executives whined about unfair competition. That threat tended to put a crimp in the WHA's style, because unfavourable opinions by the feds could mean funding cutbacks for hockey arenas. New hockey houses were absolutely critical to the existence of the new league. The WHA felt it had no choice. It, too, was forced to comply with the terms of the NHL's hands-off-youth agreement. However, team owner Nelson Skalbania knew that by openly defying the agreement and signing 17-year-old Wayne Gretzky, he would have something the NHL desperately wanted. The question was, did the NHL want it enough to merge the two leagues? Skalbania, Pocklington, and everyone else would soon find out.

Doing the Deal

When they were all inside his office, Skalbania looked at Gus Badali and boldly asked, "How much money do ya' want?"

They talked. They dickered a little. Badali had his eye on the paintings adorning the walls of Skalbania's home, but this would not be part of the deal. Peter Pocklington might be willing to give up some of his art, but Skalbania was not. Besides, money talks, and Skalbania's cash had plenty to say.

The dollars clicked into place: $100,000 for the first year, $150,000 for each of the next two years, and $175,000 for the fourth year. On top of this, there was also a signing bonus of $250,000. Over the four years, the total sum came to $825,000. That was certainly better than what Wayne's wages had been the summer before, doing road repairs for five dollars an hour.

There were smiles all around. Skalbania had done the deal, and now it was time to hold a news conference, although it wouldn't be in Indianapolis, the home of the Racers. Skalbania decided that Edmonton, a WHA town, would be the perfect place to make the signing announcement. He wanted to give the sports reporters back east something new and exciting to write about. It was also Peter Pocklington's hometown and Skalbania knew that Pocklington would love it.

However, there was still that small matter of a contract. As Skalbania's Leer jet roared away from Vancouver on its way to Edmonton, Skalbania told Wayne to write while he dictated. Wayne dug out a piece of paper, slid a lined page under a blank sheet to keep his lettering straight, clicked open his ballpoint pen, and started writing.

It was no ordinary hockey player contract. Aside from the fact that it was written in longhand aboard a Leer jet, and copied down by the player himself, this was a contract that would also be signed by Wayne's dad, who was watching all this with his wife. Wayne was too young to sign it by himself. The contract also differed in one very important way from others. It wasn't a player's contract. It was a contract for "personal services." The difference would become crucial when the leagues got together and started making rules about how many players teams could protect. In this contract, Wayne wasn't specified as a player at all.

It also wasn't specific about which team he would be playing for. Wayne might play for either Indianapolis or Houston. Skalbania liked keeping his options open. He had felt that way about buying the Houston Aeros, too. Skalbania leaned over, picked up the phone, and put a call through to Texas. The Aeros coach came on the line. Skalbania asked him what he knew about Wayne Gretzky. There was no enthusiasm on the other end of the line, just something about hearing that he didn't skate too well. Skalbania thanked him and hung up the phone. He signed the contract with Wayne Gretzky then and there but later decided to pass on purchasing the Aeros.

Eight games later, Nelson Skalbania knew that his short-term solution for Indianapolis wasn't working. He was still losing $40,000 a game. Wayne Gretzky was making a difference to the team, but he made no difference to a city that didn't really care about hockey. Skalbania phoned Wayne and gave him the news. He was going to be traded. He gave Wayne a choice: Edmonton or Winnipeg.

"Pick Edmonton," Gus Badali advised. If the NHL was going to take on any WHA teams, they would be looking not simply at the team, but at the city — the "market" the team was in. Edmonton (as Peter Pocklington knew so well) was hot. It had nothing to do with the popularity of hockey, but the oil, gas, and beef that kept the economy's temperature high.

Nelson Skalbania was not convinced. He decided they should explore possibilities in Winnipeg. Michael Gobuty was one of the Winnipeg Jets' owners. Before he made a decision, he asked others what they thought of Gretzky. Some of Gobuty's advisors were not altogether sold on the young hockey player, not for the money Skalbania was asking.

The final negotiations took place inside Gobuty's private jet. The two businessmen could not agree on the final price. Skalbania suggested they break the deadlock with a game of backgammon. Gobuty demurred. Backgammon, it seemed, was not his strong game. Skalbania shrugged. It wasn't his best game, either, but he wasn't about to tell Gobuty that. This was all about gamesmanship. They left Winnipeg without a deal.

Their next stop was Edmonton.

Like Nelson Skalbania a few months before, Pocklington

hadn't seen Wayne play. He asked his new coach, Glen Sather, if they wanted him. Sather had seen Wayne play, all right. At first, he hadn't been all that impressed. Then the coach had watched as the young, fast Indianapolis Racer had lived up to his team's name. Wayne had zipped around an Oilers defenceman and put the puck in the net. Had he just been lucky? That question was answered a mere 39 seconds later, when Gretzky raced down the ice and scored again. Sather took a harder look and made a mental note to get this kid if he could. Now, suddenly, the owner was handing him the opportunity. Sather didn't hesitate. He told Pocklington to buy Gretzky.

The deal included $300,000 in cash and a $250,000 note to be applied against the $500,000 Pocklington promised to pay Skalbania, should the NHL accept the Oilers into the fold. Caught short of cash a little later, Pocklington bought back his $250,000 note from Nelson Skalbania for just $100,000. In the end, Wayne Gretzky had become an Edmonton Oilers player for just $400,000.

A few months later, on Wayne Gretzky's 18th birthday, a little on-the-ice party was held for him at Northlands Coliseum. There was a cake, a bottle of bubbly, and a contract sitting on a small table set up for the benefit of photographers and fans. What Wayne signed that night was the longest and richest agreement in professional hockey history — a 21-year contract worth $3 million over the first 10 years alone. Wayne wouldn't be a player, you understand. Pocklington had adopted the Skalbania strategy.

"This contract is for personal services," he told the media. "There's no way anyone's going to touch him when we join the NHL."

Chapter 4
Building the Team

fter his halcyon days as a Memorial Cup winning Edmonton Oil Kings player back in 1961-62, Glen Sather had endured the long and winding major league road travelled by hundreds of other long-forgotten NHL journeymen. When the remnants of the Oil Kings became the new Alberta Oilers, Glen Sather thought he might play for Bill Hunter once again. Hunter drafted him but couldn't sign him. However, Detroit did. Nonetheless, Sather was not destined to play in Hockeytown but rather in Memphis, Tennessee, earning 48 points and 98 penalties. He might not have been a scorer, but he was a scrapper. At the very least, the time he had spent in the penalty box had been impressive.

Memphis was merely his first stop on that seemingly

endless road of NHL near-fame. Other stops: Oklahoma City, Boston (where Sather played two seasons and 13 playoff games without scoring one single point), and then Pittsburgh. He arrived in New York for the 1971-72 season, just as the Rangers became a Stanley Cup contender. Ironically, the Rangers played the Bruins, who took the Cup, and with it, any chances Glen Sather had of wearing that special ring. Glen hit the road again, bound for St. Louis, and after that, Montreal (one year too soon for their Cup series) and then Minnesota.

By 1975, 32-year-old Glen Sather was skating for an expansion team that would win only 20 games that season. Sather helped, posting nine markers and 10 assists. Just as the next season began, Edmonton — which had never dealt away his rights — came calling. It was time to go home.

Suddenly, newcomer Glen Sather was the Oilers captain. Then almost as suddenly — when it appeared that the Oilers would be edged out of the 1976-77 playoffs — Glen was offered the coach's job. "Offered" is putting it politely. The general manager, Bep Guidolin, told him that he could either watch the game from behind the bench (already setting Sather up as the scapegoat for another bad season), or watch it as a fan from behind the glass. Sather thought the space behind the bench looked just fine. Then, a miracle of sorts occurred. The Oilers won enough games — nine — to secure a playoff spot. However, they blew the semi-finals, losing five games to Houston. Peter Pocklington may not have liked what he saw on the ice during that series, but he certainly liked what — and who — he saw behind the bench. And so Glen Sather stayed and Pocklington sacked the GM instead.

The Beginning of the End

Early in the summer of 1977, as the Oilers' new coach attempted to put together some kind of plan for the coming season, leaders of the two leagues were cloistered in New York, attempting to forge some kind of merger. Three days of heated meetings had, it seemed, resulted in an acceptable formula. Six WHA teams would join the NHL and have a chance at the Stanley Cup. What did this mean to the Oilers? What impact would the decision have on the team roster? The questions were set aside for an even more important one: would the Oilers even exist by September? Then came more news from New York. If Edmonton was still playing next season, it would be as a WHA team. The proposed merger was off, killed by six intractable NHL owners.

So tenuous was the Oilers' lease on life that summer that the WHA drew up two 1977-78 schedules, one for eight teams and another for seven. When Peter Pocklington decided they were in, Glen Sather went to work again. One unpleasant task was to compensate for the loss of defenceman Robin Sadler, who turned his back on a two-year, $200,000 contract to return to B.C. and become a fireman. Sadler had not been enjoying himself. Sather could have told him that he wasn't the only one.

Glen Sather's first full season was just slightly better

than the previous one. Winning 38 games and tying three in an 80-game schedule, the Oilers placed fifth and qualified for a berth in the playoffs for the Avco Cup. Then, the father-son team of Gordie and Mark Howe came to town, along with the rest of the second-place New England Whalers, to show Oilers fans what real hockey was all about. In this particular series, real hockey was about winning four games out of five, which New England did very handily. The Whalers went on to meet the Jets in Cup competition. The Oilers went home for the holidays. It was another long summer for Sather as he prepared for the season to come.

Two circumstances made the next season particularly significant for the Oilers. One was the arrival of Wayne Gretzky in November 1979. Gretzky didn't come alone. He was part of a three-player deal. Also purchased from Nelson Skalbania were the Racers' young, promising goaltender Eddie Mio and sharp-shooting left-winger Peter Driscoll. That gave Glen Sather and the team more to play with. Nevertheless, the challenges continued. Earlier, Sather had courted Butch Goring of the L.A. Kings. The Oilers made what Goring called "a great offer." The Kings saw the Oilers and raised them, offering Goring US$250,000 for each of the next five years. He decided to stay in California.

Undeterred by that disappointment and others, Sather concentrated on developing the team, bolstering its defensive side so it could make sudden, offensive attacks to be led by Wayne Gretzky. Sometimes, from behind the bench, Sather

Wayne Gretzky

seemed ready to participate in those attacks himself. Although he was a prankster with his own squad, he demonstrated his old competitive streak from behind the bench. During games he quickly turned tough, yelling put-downs at opposing players as they skated by, and offering tart and pointed replies to comments shouted at him by the other team's fans.

It is easy to think of 1978-79 as "the Gretzky season," but another, bigger event was about to change everything for Glen Sather and Peter Pocklington. The 1978-79 season was to be the last one for the World Hockey Association. Encouraged by Nelson Skalbania's deal with young Wayne, which acted as a finger-in-the-eye to the NHL, Birmingham's John Bassett upped the ante and signed seven juniors. Obviously, the WHA was not taking the NHL's threats seriously. What it was taking, instead, were the young, talented players that an ever-expanding NHL would need to infuse new energy into its future.

Almost unbelievably, the Edmonton Oilers finished the season as league leaders. True, the WHA was just a six-team league (Houston and Indianapolis were gone before the season ended), but Edmonton's 48-30-2 season standing was Glen Sather's best yet. There was even more to celebrate. Edmonton's new found energy and aggressiveness gave the Oilers a seven-game victory over New England in the Avco Cup playoffs. Edmonton faced two-time, Cup-winning Winnipeg in the finals.

The first two games of the finals were played in Edmonton, but fewer fans showed up for each game than paid to see the average regular season game. As the puck went down on the first face-off of game three in Winnipeg, there were still plenty of seats available. The attention of hockey fans was on that "other series" between Stanley Cup competitors, Montreal Canadiens and New York Rangers.

There was another underlying reason for fan apathy: many feared this was the end. The concerns about the league's future had infested other teams, too. Many players went into the finals with doubts and misgivings. Where would they be this time next year?

The Oilers lost the first two games on home ice and were finally goaded into action by the high-scoring Gretzky to win 8-3 in the third game. The Great One scored the opening goal in game four and another in the second period to break a 1-1 tie. However, the Jets beat Oilers goalie Dave Dryden two more times to give Winnipeg a close 3-2 win. The Oilers roared back in game five, beating the Jets 10-2. Game six was an almost equally lopsided affair, ending with a 7-3 Avco Cup victory for the Jets. Thousands came out to cheer the champs as they rolled slowly down Main Street in Winnipeg, although many lining the parade route seemed to be cheering for something else. One banner read, "Next Year, the Stanley Cup."

The NHL held another vote to decide whether the two leagues would merge. With the voting complete, the 14-3 result was uncontestable. The contentious and costly contest between the two professional leagues was finally over. As a consequence, the WHA was history. In the end, the two leagues didn't call it a merger. They called it, more accurately, an NHL expansion. Only four of the strongest WHA teams would join the NHL: the Quebec Nordiques, the New England Whalers, the Winnipeg Jets, and the Edmonton Oilers. How did Edmonton hockey fans feel about the announcement of their new NHL team? The answer was unequivocal: they snapped up 15,242 season tickets in just 11 days — every single ticket available.

Those ticket revenues would soon come in handy. Edmonton — like other WHA-turned-NHL cities — would pay dearly for the privilege of inclusion in the one-and-only league. The price of admission was $6 million. There was another cost, too: manpower. Players in the four former WHA teams were soon up for grabs in a "reclamation" draft.

It is a testimony to the excellence of the Oilers' lineup that NHL teams took many players from its promising roster. Twelve players who had taken the team to the finals were lost, including, at first, Ed Mio and Dave Dryden. That left the Oilers without a starting goalie. With players taken from wing, centre, and especially defence, there wasn't a position that didn't suffer losses, either to league redistribution or to retirement. However, after more than a year of league indecision, at last Glen Sather knew exactly where he stood: up to his neck in team reconstruction. His first order of business was to retrieve the best of those who had been lost.

Team Builder

It could have been worse. With a keen eye and razor-sharp strategy, Sather recaptured some of his high-scoring players, including second- and third-place point-getters, right-winger Blair MacDonald, and centre Brett Callighen. Then he managed to snatch back goalies Eddie Mio and Dave Dryden.

Of the 16 players Sather selected during the expansion draft that soon followed, only four made the roster — defencemen Pat Price (from the New York Islanders), Lee Fogolin (from Buffalo), and Doug Hicks (from Chicago). Pittsburgh Penguins player Colin Campbell (destined to become the New York Rangers' coach) would have a brief, one-season stay in Edmonton. Sather's personal reclamation program also brought back Risto Siltanen and Oilers tough-guy Dave Semenko. Sather and his scout Barry Fraser then began to formulate their strategy for the entry draft in August.

In the first round of the next draft, the Edmonton Oilers would pick 21st from a long roster of promising players from the Oshawa Generals, Lethbridge Broncos, Niagara Falls Flyers, and other training-ground teams. The list was considerably shorter by the time Fraser announced the Oilers' choices. It was one of the prices to be paid for entry into the NHL. Former WHA teams were relegated to the final pick positions. Already gone were great players that included Duane Sutter, Rob Ramage, Mike Gartner, and Ray Bourque. Finally, number 21 was announced and the Oilers picked Kevin Lowe of the Quebec Remparts. Sather called Lowe's mother and told her that he was "thrilled to have him."

Acquiring Lowe had been no snap decision. That's not the way Sather and Fraser worked. The actual draft was the end of the selection process. Weeks before, names had been discussed and lists had been made. Lowe rated high with Fraser.

"We had him eleventh on our list," Fraser said later. "When his name came up, we didn't think about it for a minute." They didn't think about it on that particular day, anyway. On draft day, the scouting, the interviewing, and the thinking had already been done.

The Oilers had given up their second-round pick in order to retrieve Semenko. Then came the third round, with a 48th pick. Edmonton chose a player who had escaped the serious notice of other scouts. That was understandable — in 52 WHA games, he had just one goal and 10 assists. So, why were the Oilers interested? The answer to that went back to the previous March, when Sather had first seen him play. The kid was big, strong, and good in the corners. Sather told others that if Mark Messier was available in the summer, he would "take him in a minute." Soon, Messier was part of the team.

Then came the fourth round. The decision had already been made, although it hadn't been a quick one. Urged to look closely at Glenn Anderson, Sather asked Fraser if he knew what he was doing. "This kid is going to be in the Hall of Fame someday," was the scout's self-assured reply. Fraser had seen the 19-year-old from B.C. do it all at the Canadian Olympic team's training camp. He knew Anderson excelled at scoring, playmaking, and speed skating.

Sather was convinced. He urged the tall, speedy goal-getter to join them immediately. At first, Anderson hesitated. He wanted to finish the national team program first. Fortunately, that wasn't going to be a problem for the Oilers

— they would happily wait for a talent this promising.

The following year, at the Montreal Forum, where 2500 fascinated spectators attended the first public draft, Sather and Fraser put two cornerstones of their future Stanley Cup winning team into place. In the first round, in a sixth pick, Sather chose the Kitchener Rangers' Paul Coffey. Coffey was the kind of offensive defenceman Oilers team-builders were looking for. In The Great One's opinion, he had "maybe more speed than any defenceman who ever lived."

In the fourth round, Sather and Fraser had the opportunity to pick someone else they had been looking for — and had found — sometime before. Subtle scouting and an excellent eye for talent had put Finnish Olympic team member Jari Kurri on their list months before. The Oilers had to wait until Kurri won the silver medal in the 1980 World Junior Championships, but the wait — as with Anderson — would be worth it.

"We could never have waited until the fourth round if everybody knew what we knew," Fraser chuckled. "He'd have gone real high." It was another Sather steal.

Halfway through the first NHL season, goalie Dave Dryden retired. A fast trade with Quebec meant that Ron Chipperfield would be replaced with starter goalie Ron Low. The coach and the scout were still looking for more netminding talent and found it in Victoria, B.C. and, of all places, Billings, Montana. They had watched Grant Fuhr play a number of times for the Victoria Cougars and had carefully

Paul Coffey

studied Billings Bighorn goalie, Andy Moog. Moog became an Oilers player in the sixth pick of that year's draft, and in the 1981 amateur draft, Fuhr joined the team. In training camp, Fuhr was so good that Sather sent Andy Moog down to Wichita in the Central League for a brief remedial stint.

Finally, in the spring of 1981, Pat Price was traded for another player Sather had lost back in the insanity of the reclamation draft: right-winger Pat Hughes.

They were all energetic, talented men with great potential. Now what was Glen Sather going to do with them?

Style Setter

Acquiring Wayne Gretzky or other strong players didn't represent a "Sather strategy" as such. It was merely the initial phase of a bigger, more ambitious one. The next phase meant building a team around his key offensive star — but what kind of team, and what kind of play?

Then, as now, attitudes were influenced by conventional wisdom. In the 1970s — the era of the goon — intimidation and threats of violence from the brawlers-and-maulers were common tactics. Wayne Gretzky, for one, was no fighter, and he certainly didn't need to be. What Glen Sather was about to do was flaunt conventional wisdom. In this, he was not alone.

"What's the league waiting for, somebody to die out there?" protested L.A. Kings' marksman Marcel Dionne.

The Montreal Canadiens — those kings of finesse — had led the way in 1976, defeating the league's self-appointed intimidators, the Philadelphia Flyers, to win the Stanley Cup. The Habs' victory over Philadelphia's "Broad Street Bullies" was, as Serge Savard put it, "a victory for hockey."

A change was in the air.

There was also a lesson to be learned from the three-time Avco Cup winning Winnipeg Jets. In its last two seasons, the Winnipeg Jets had put as many as eight Europeans on its player roster. This might have been foresight on the part of the Jets' organization, but more than likely it was simply desperation. Up against the NHL's financial clout, penny-pinching WHA teams were forced to get their players from anywhere they could — including overseas.

Glen Sather had been impressed with the likes of Anders Hedberg, Ulf Nilsson, and other European players in the WHA. The point, Glen Sather knew, was not to import these players and then attempt to retrain them to play North American style hockey. To some extent, the Jets embraced a European style — a winning style — of playing. That was another point not lost on Glen Sather. He liked the style and he liked winning. In 1979, during a trip to Finland and Sweden, he found more to like. He especially liked what he saw as he watched youngsters play peewee hockey. He liked the swift passing, the sudden switching of sides, and the use of attacking defencemen. Glen Sather brought it all back with him — the flow, the finesse, and most of all, the speed-skating offence.

Now, it seemed, he had some players who might master the style, and, by the 1980-81 season, three that already had: Finnish centre Matti Hagman, left-wing Jari Kurri, and defenceman Risto Siltanen.

Managing the Team and the Media

The ideal situation for a team-builder such as Glen Sather was to undertake the construction work in relative obscurity. Perfecting plays based on innovative strategies was best done in secret. Not only did a lack of outside attention help focus energy and effort, but it allowed the strategies to remain safe, even when executed before thousands of spectators. Used against different teams in different places, these strategies were rarely fully realized in single — or even consecutive — games.

Fortunately during this time, the press helped Sather out by providing almost no coverage of the fledgling Edmonton team. Sports writers were too busy writing and voicing their opinions about Montreal, Boston, New York, and Philadelphia — the Stanley Cup contenders of the era. In 1978 and 1979, the glare of the media spotlight was brightest in the biggest of the big-league cities. Out in the west, Edmonton was an ideal construction site, where Sather, Gretzky, Messier, and the rest skated in relative obscurity. It wouldn't be until later, in the early 1980s, that the Oilers, and especially Wayne Gretzky, would sweat under the full heat of the media lamp.

In September, new arrivals who had been drafted from minor league teams earlier in the spring congregated in Wild Bill Hunter's nondescript Edmonton Gardens for rookie camp. The rookies were carefully scrutinized, with observations recorded in Barry Fraser's "Player Evaluation Report." Each rookie's skills — skating, puck handling, passing, checking, and more than 70 other components were rated on a scale of one to nine. There was the rare "one" ("reject"), but more than a few "two's" ("reject with one good quality"). Most merited an overall three or four. The season before, Wayne Gretzky had scored a nine. Sather, Fraser, and assistant coach Bryan Watson weren't the only ones watching.

The veterans straggled into the Gardens to see the new guys play (a single season in the professional league qualified you as a mature player in this outfit). Sitting at rink side, these wise, old pros would shake their heads, smile, and snicker. A week later, the smiles were gone as Watson put them through their grueling paces at the veterans' camp in Jasper. It was no laughing matter.

As a master strategist and planner, Sather was prepared when the media shifted focus a season or two later (and then felt foolish, when Edmonton blew the first-round 1982 playoffs to L.A.). In the early days, those who travelled to Edmonton, including the media, found themselves quickly won over by the adroit and charming Oilers manager.

To the players, Glen Sather was many things. He was fair, taking a player aside to let him know how he felt about an abysmal level of play, rather than chewing him out in front of his teammates. He could also be quietly ruthless, often in a particularly creative way. One year, Mark Messier had arrived at the wrong airport in Edmonton for a flight with the team. He called Sather to say he would be late. Sather told him that was no problem — he'd find a ticket waiting at the counter when he arrived at the right airport. The team would fly on ahead. Messier got the ticket all right, destination: Wichita, Kansas, where the Oilers' Houston farm team was playing. Sather let Messier suffer for his mistake, setting him adrift for close to two weeks before throwing him a lifeline.

They called Sather "Slats." He was a prankster. By all accounts, in those early days, Glen "Slats" Sather made it fun: buckets of cold water for the guys as they took hot showers, shaving cream in their hairbrushes, and talcum powder sprinkled in their hairdryers. He was also generous (he and Anne Sather had hosted Wayne Gretzky during his first three weeks in Edmonton), offered plenty of praise, and was clear about his expectations.

"One day we're gonna be in the NHL," Sather told Wayne not long after he arrived, "and one day you are going to be captain of this hockey team. Remember I told you that."

He was also a benign manipulator. No surprise: Slats had studied psychology in college.

Gretzky had long-since moved out of the Sather home and was rooming with veteran Ace Bailey and his wife. Kevin Lowe, on the other hand was new, alone, and away from Quebec for the first time. Sather suggested Gretzky and Lowe get together (although "ordered" is the more accurate term, as Lowe remembered). It worked. Gretzky was an eating machine and Lowe, ironically, was a terrific cook. Even better, teammates Doug Hicks and Dave Lumley lived next door. Mark Messier would drive down from his parents' home in nearby St. Albert to hang out. Glen Sather must have smiled. Not all teamwork is forged in the arena.

Later, Kevin Lowe remembered how positive Sather was. More than positive, he could be downright inspirational. On the eve of the finals with the New York Islanders, the team was tense. For months, the players had been reliving the agony of a resounding defeat and the loss of the Stanley Cup the year before. Sather could sense the paranoia.

"You guys are the best team in the NHL!" he exhorted. "If you just use your heads and play the way we're telling you to play, you're going to win and you're going to win easy." It wasn't just what he said, it was the way he said it.

"When he spoke I got goose bumps," recalled Lowe. "I wanted to get out onto the ice right away."

It was psychology at work.

Chapter 5
Growing Pains

alfway through that first 1979-80 NHL season, Edmonton was third from the bottom of the standings. It was time for a shakedown. Some of the "shaking" went on between the older Oilers players and the newcomers. Sure, Wayne Gretzky was good, but so what? He needed to be better. That was the way veteran defenceman Pat Price and goalie Jim Craig figured it, and they both told Wayne so. As Gretzky skated near the crease, a frustrated Craig, smarting from a two-goal deficit, snarled, "Gretzky, just who do you think you are, anyway?"

Gretzky, it seemed, knew exactly who he was. In the next half hour, he scored three goals to win the game. Both Price and Craig were gone from the team within a couple of seasons.

Six games from the end of the season, the team rallied and were within one spot of qualifying for the playoffs. Messier's brief stay down in Houston was the kind of "shakedown" maneuver that, although not planned, had had a positive effect not only on Mark, but on his teammates, too. The second was the trade that had brought goalie Ron Low west from the Quebec Nordiques. Low regularly made great plays in the crease. All his teammates on the ice had to do was put the puck past the other goalie, which they were already doing with increasing regularity.

Later that year, Gretzky made it clear again who he thought he was — someone out to beat Marcel Dionne in the scoring race. In Edmonton's final (and winning) regular season game against Colorado, it wasn't looking good until Wayne assisted on the tying goal and shot in the game-winning marker, his 51st. Gretzky had little trouble with Sather's offensive concept — 51 goals and 137 points were proof of that.

His team had needed the win against Colorado, because now they were in the playoffs, but Wayne figured he still needed the points, even though he had racked up 23 of them in the last 11 games. What he really needed was at least one more goal, because at the end of the night, after the Kings had played their game, and all the goals and assists were added together, both Dionne (53-84-137) and Gretzky (51-86-137) claimed 137 points. The player to break the tie would be the one who had scored the most goals. That meant Dionne would carry away the Art Ross Trophy. Wayne's consolation prizes: the Lady Byng, for most sportsmanlike player, and the coveted Hart Trophy, as most valuable player.

The Three-Game Playoffs

Edmonton was a new team in the playoffs, and there was a new rule for them to play by. The Oilers would play a first-time, best-of-five preliminary round series. Early in the second half of the season, there was little doubt which team they might meet after the regular season. For months, the Oilers had been watching a tough bunch of grinders and goal-getters with a blend of disbelief and dismay. By late winter, the Philadelphia Flyers had played 53 consecutive games without a defeat.

"It was a magical ride," said the new Flyers coach, Pat Quinn, in wonder.

However, the string of victories had ended abruptly with a seven-game losing streak, just about the time the Oilers finally took off. The Flyers posted a lacklustre 3-5-5 in their last 13 games of the season. Maybe there was hope.

"We were scared bleepless going into the playoffs," recalled Philly goalie Phil Myre. Oh, if the Oilers had only known!

Game one was a seesaw affair. Edmonton battled back after an early, two-goal deficit, after Ron Low belatedly found his confidence in the crease. The Oilers took a third period 3-2 lead. A 30-foot drive by Flyers player Rick MacLeish evened the score. Eight minutes into overtime, Flyers captain Bobby Clarke bounced the puck off Low's pad and into the net. The second game was an even more decisive 5-1 Flyers' victory. In the third game, spurred on by screaming fans in Edmonton, the Oilers pulled ahead with goals by Messier and Gretzky in the first. Then it was overtime again, when Ken Linseman circled around Oilers defenceman Pat Price, and beat Ron Low for the winning 3-2 victory. Suddenly, after a brief, first-round, three-game playoff series, the Edmonton Oilers' first NHL season was over.

Two Steps Forward ...

... was followed by one step back, or so it seemed in those early Oilers seasons.

As the 1980-81 season began, the team was still in its formative stage, with individuals learning to play, and in some cases to live, with each other. It was even tougher for the team's trio of Finns. Kurri barely spoke English. The language barrier tended to make the Finns a team-within-a-team. Glen Sather knew it, although he didn't have time to dwell on it. He was happy enough that Jari and Wayne both spoke the language of hockey fluently. Then there was the duo of Kevin Lowe and Lee Fogolin. It was as if those two were joined at the hip out on the ice. That was the way it should be for two defencemen, and that was the way Glen liked it.

The "Glen-and-Barry" headhunting team was in high gear. There were more bright newcomers. Defenceman Paul

Coffey was so unsure about how long he would be putting on an Oilers uniform that he was still living at the Edmonton Plaza Hotel. Right-winger Curt Brackenbury had come from the Quebec Nordiques just a few weeks before.

The Oilers were the youngest gang in the NHL. Few were married. As the second, big-league season began, Coffey, Gretzky, and Messier were still teenagers. Jari Kurri was barely 20, Kevin Lowe was just 21, and Risto Siltanen was 22. Twenty-five-year-old defenceman Lee Fogolin, Doug Hicks (a league veteran of eight years), and captain Blair MacDonald, 26, were decidedly middle-aged by comparison. Goalie Ron Low — at age 30 — appeared to be the team's designated "old man."

"Who was your childhood idol?" an interviewer asked right-winger Glenn Anderson.

"Wayne Gretzky," the wisecracking 20-year-old Anderson replied.

At the beginning of that season, they were playing badly. Twenty-one teams were eligible for a shot in the play-offs that year. That meant just five teams — the league's very worst — would be out of the running. It looked like the Oilers would be one of them. Even at that early stage of the season, it was time to stop thinking and start doing.

Glen Sather took a deep breath and then took stock. Maybe it was time to get rid of a few players. The team was playing so badly that the recently promoted general manager and president wondered whether it was only players he needed to get rid of. Maybe he needed to get rid of coach Bryan Watson, too. That would be tough. Bugsy was a good friend.

First, however, it was back to the minors for a handful of players. Then, after the team lost nine out of 10 home games, Sather and Pocklington said goodbye to Bryan Watson — with two years' salary to cushion the blow. Assistant coach Billy Harris would stay exactly where he was. The former Toronto mainstay had skated for the mighty Leafs in the 1950s and 1960s and had seen a lot of Stanley Cup action. If there was one thing this club needed, it was people who had seen a little of that and knew what it was like to go all the way. Glen Sather decided not to go coach shopping. Instead, he walked out of the front office and moved back in behind the bench. That's how bad things were.

As September moved through October and into November, things didn't get much better. After a brief flurry of victories, including, to the delight of hometown fans, a 10-3 win over Chicago, the Oilers lost eight of the next nine games. That winter, Edmonton couldn't even beat teams it was *supposed* to beat — ones in the bottom half of the standings. They were whipped by Minnesota and then beaten by Washington.

The team was plagued by injuries. Injured earlier in the season, Ron Low's hand had healed at last. Then, during a warm-up with the farm team, the puck smashed his hand — the *same* hand. Low shaved his beard off in disgust and sat out the rest of the season. In January, the Oilers were beaten badly 5-0 by the Montreal Canadiens. That hurt, but for Eddie Mio, the pain was physical. He was carried out on a stretcher after Rejean Houle sent the puck crashing into his facemask.

Inexplicably, however, in the midst of all these horrors, the Oilers were able to shellack the Canadiens 9-1 on home ice a few weeks later. There was no doubt that the Oilers had something going for them. Too bad they couldn't find it more often.

The new coach began retooling his team. As winter moved into spring that second NHL season, there were more goodbyes (including Dave Semenko, Don Murdoch, Ron Low, and later captain Blair "BJ" MacDonald). Some were gone just briefly and some forever.

Mark Messier was on Sather's list of trades. In hindsight, because we know what Messier eventually achieved, this seems shocking. However, at the time, nobody knew for sure what he could do, although Sather had a pretty good idea. He also knew Messier was nowhere close to achieving his potential. Sather couldn't afford to wait. He had a long talk with Mark. The word "demotion" might not have been overtly mentioned, but the possibility was certainly there. Messier was told to stay home at night and reminded about Sather's famous bed check.

While on the road, nobody knew when Glen would check the players' beds. The season before, big Dave Semenko had tiptoed down the hotel corridor one hour past the eleven o'clock curfew, opened the door of his room, and found Slats sitting inside, grinning up at him. "And did you have a good night?" was all the coach said before he quietly let himself out.

After the conversation with Sather, Mark went home and had a long conversation with himself. By mid-February, he was a changed player.

At this point in the season, some of the players were starting to come around, and some of the best ones were getting even better (Wayne Gretzky had just posted 100 points), but the team itself still needed some work. Unfortunately, the NHL wasn't about to give the Oilers — or any team — time off to improve their performance. It was time to "face the music," so to speak. The team was about to play the St. Louis Blues.

The Blues were the league's number-one team. They had won 24 of their last 27 games, and boasted netminder Mike Liut as one of their own — the man many were already calling the season's MVP.

In the second period, with the score tied 2-2, things began to happen. Right-winger Curt Brackenbury hammered a shot at the St. Louis goal. Liut made the save, but, as usual, Wayne Gretzky anticipated the rebound. He pounced on the puck, zipped it past Liut, and the Oilers pulled ahead. Mark Messier and Glenn Anderson then worked together to make it 4-2. On the bench, the Oilers' tension started to ease. In the third period, captain BJ MacDonald dropped the puck back to Paul Coffey, who dashed over the blue line and backhanded it past an increasingly frustrated Liut to make the score 5-2.

Then, something miraculous happened. People who were in the stands that night remember it and still talk about it. Wayne Gretzky put in another one. Barely nine seconds later, he followed it up with one more. The crowd was on its feet, applauding wildly. Liut acknowledged Wayne's feat in his own way, by simply skating off the ice. As Liut's replacement, Ed Staniowski, hunkered down between the pipes, you had to wonder, just what he was thinking? If he thought the worst was over, he was wrong.

Fewer than three minutes passed before Gretzky put in another goal. The kid wouldn't — or couldn't — stop. He shot in another one! Were these the fastest four consecutive goals in NHL history? At the time, nobody knew for sure, but the record Wayne Gretzky tied that night — most goals in a single period — had been set 47 long years before by Leafs player Harvey "Busher" Jackson (in some ways, the Wayne Gretzky of his day).

The Oilers won that night. In 1981, any win was a great win for the Oilers. But this wasn't just any win, and St. Louis wasn't just any team. The Oilers had just whipped the number one team in the league, 9-2.

After handing the Blues that crushing defeat, the Oilers went on to win only four of the next 10 games. The victories were fabulous, rekindling faith in the team, but many of the defeats were humiliating. Where was the consistency?

Getting Better

At the beginning of the season, the Oilers had basically been, "Wayne Gretzky and those other guys." By early March, however, there were half a dozen new sports celebrities wearing white, blue, and orange. They had names people knew and spoke of with conviction and excitement: Messier, Coffey, Anderson, Moog, Kurri, and Lowe. There was talk about "the team of the future." However, right now, there was another playoff series coming up. This one was against the Montreal Canadiens.

The Oilers didn't have to look at the Canadiens' roster to know who they were up against. They knew these men. They were winners of four straight Stanley Cups: Guy Lafleur, Steve Shutt, Serge Savard, and Guy Lapointe. Back in Montreal, the playoffs were a given; the Cup victory simply expected. It was an annual cultural tradition. This was the team Edmonton faced. This was the team that a basically unproven goalie faced. This was Andy Moog's moment. As it turned out, it was also the team's moment.

Inside the Forum, the Habs' holy shrine, youthful Oilers dashed around aging superstars. The first game was a decisive win: Oilers 6, Canadiens 3. In game two, Coffey and Siltanen scored in the first two periods, giving the Oilers a one-marker lead. The Canadiens watched as all but one of their 30 shots were turned aside by Andy Moog. Kurri found the Montreal net again in the third period to make it a 3-1 victory for the Oilers.

"We Believe in Miracles" read the huge banner on the wall of Northlands Coliseum, inviting ticket holders inside for game three. Over 17,000 Edmonton believers chanted "Andy! Andy! Andy!" and watched Moog play a thrilling game of "keep out," while teammates, spurred on by a Gretzky hat trick, humiliated the Habs 6-2. The front page of the *Edmonton Sun* simply repeated what everybody else was saying: "INCREDIBLE!"

In Unionville, New York, during the next series, the Islanders brought the high-flying Edmonton squad back down to earth. It was a bumpy landing, with a pair of 8-2 and 6-3 losses for Edmonton. Back in Edmonton, again inspired by a Gretzky hat trick, the Oilers beat the Islanders 5-2. A 4-4 tie sent game four into overtime but Islanders defenceman Ken Morrow tipped the puck in past Andy Moog at 5:41. The Long Island crowd held its collective breath as the Oilers moved ahead 4-2 in game five, then cheered as their home team closed the gap 4-3. Four minutes before the end of the game, the singing began on the Oilers' bench.

"Here we go Oilers, here we go! Here we go! Here we go Oilers, here we go!"

Glen Sather shrugged and laughed. It seemed that every time the team got into trouble, they'd start to sing. That was okay by him.

"I think it was Mark Messier who started it," Paul Coffey recalled. "It just felt right to start singing," he remembered, laughing. Andy Moog kept the puck out during those last, long minutes of the game. Imagine that: the Canadian youngsters would be going back to "Edmonchuck," dragging the Stanley Cup champs along with them for game six.

The Oilers held the Islanders at bay until into the second period, and then the 1-1 tie slipped away. Mark Messier put Edmonton on the scoreboard again, but the Islanders Bryan Trottier and Dave Langevin put Gretzky against the boards while Denis Potvin and Mike Bossy put the puck past Andy Moog. When the game ended 5-2, so did the Oilers' chances at the Stanley Cup.

Wayne Gretzky was truly disappointed. Yet, there were compensations. He won his second Hart Trophy as most valuable player by five votes (Mike Liut, the runner-up had his own disappointments), and, at last, he had beaten Marcel Dionne in the scoring race 164-135.

"Gretzky makes me feel like an old man," said the Kings sharpshooter with a sigh.

Chapter 6
The Turnaround

For Andy Moog, it was one of the worst things that could have happened. Just weeks after his playoff triumph against Montreal and his outstanding showing against the powerhouse New York Islanders, his future was threatened by a newcomer to his own team. His name was Grant Fuhr.

The Final Offensive Play

What Sather the strategist wanted was a goalie so rock solid that the Oilers defencemen — especially Paul Coffey — no longer felt compelled to hang back to protect a lead or stem an attack. The defencemen needed to feel free to dash up the ice and join the offence. Fuhr, Sather felt, was that goalie. Moog was still extremely valuable, a key component in the two-goalie system that fast, furious hockey demanded. So, Moog wasn't going anywhere. And that, he eventually realized, was the problem. For the rest of his career with the Oilers, Moog would live life in the shadow cast by the great Grant Fuhr. In four seasons, Moog would perform in only 11 playoff games.

Watching rookie Fuhr in that first season, assistant coach Billy Harris was reminded of the poise and cool of legendary Maple Leafs netminder Johnny Bower. Considering that Johnny was a 10-year pro in his 30s during his NHL rookie year and Fuhr was barely 20, fresh from the minors, this was high praise, indeed. Fuhr's style was something of a throwback, too. In peewee hockey, the Alberta-born Fuhr had been coached by "Mr. Goalie," the great Glenn Hall, who had won his Stanley Cup ring with the Chicago Blackhawks 20 years before. Living a quiet, retired life on his farm, Hall had taught Fuhr his trademark butterfly style.

Fuhr's toughness was exceptional. When the pressure was on, or when the score was close, Grant Fuhr didn't merely reach out to snag the puck with his glove or knock it aside with his stick. He would *lunge* for it. He would commit his entire body to keeping the rubber out of the crease. A man with incredible hand-eye coordination, he routinely made miraculous saves.

His temperament was puzzling. Gretzky wondered more than once if he ever got excited. Nothing seemed to rattle Grant Fuhr. Errors by defencemen might cost the team goals and

Grant Fuhr

Fuhr his statistics, but he never berated his teammates. Before big games, you wouldn't have found him slumped in the dressing room, moody and morose, or chattering away nervously. Instead, Fuhr could be found striding across the golf course, a smile on his face. "It clears the head," he would say.

Before long, the Oilers had the confidence to play a hell-bent-for-leather, cowboy-style offence. They knew they had a "pardner" back in their own zone who would "keep the barn door closed." Now they could take chances and be riskier in their play. More and more, it was fast-skating, quick-passing defenceman Paul Coffey who led the charge into enemy territory. Glen Sather was a happy man, while stoic Andy Moog remained patient and understanding … at least for the time being.

Gretzky's Personal Best

Just seven games into the 1981-82 season, lantern-jawed Mark Messier told reporters that his team would finish first in their division. That meant beating Vancouver and Colorado, the team's Alberta rivals, the Calgary Flames, and the L.A. Kings. Reporters were skeptical.

All the major players on the team started scoring well, doing their bit to help Messier make good on his prediction. None did as much as The Great One. During the Oilers' 39th game of the season, Wayne Gretzky scored four times against the Philadelphia Flyers in Northlands Coliseum. It was the fourth goal — a quick shot three seconds before the final siren — that really counted, not so much for the game they had already won minutes before, but for the record book.

Gretzky had started his internal countdown at the beginning of the game, as had most of the crowd. The first goal was number 47 of the season, the second was number

48, and the third, number 49. Then, as the clock continued ticking, there was nothing for about 10 minutes. Gretzky was desperate. Grant Fuhr stopped a loose shot and pushed it toward Glenn Anderson at the red line. Gretzky dashed past him.

"Pass it to me! Pass it to me!" he shouted. Anderson did as he was told.

With most of the crowd on its feet, Wayne pelted up the ice, fired, and watched Philly netminder Pete Peeters go sprawling as the puck hit the back of the net. By scoring his 50th goal in the 39th game, The Great One had bettered the 50-goals-in-50-games record set almost 40 years before by Maurice "Rocket" Richard. Mark Messier and the rest of the players mobbed Wayne before he could skate off the ice.

For many who had been watching Wayne for years, this moment came as no surprise. Seven years before, back in Sault Ste. Marie, one of the owners of the Soo Greyhounds had placed a long-distance call to his professional hockey-playing son. The son's name was Phil Esposito.

"There's a boy here who will break all your records one day," Esposito's father had told him. "He's only 14 and he's playing Junior in the Soo. His name is Gretzky. Wayne Gretzky."

At the time, Esposito had been dubious. "Well, that's great, dad. But he's only 14. Let's wait and see."

Even before the game, fans had stopped speculating about 50-in-50 (the feat seemed fairly likely) and had started speculating about Gretzky's ability to equal Phil Esposito's league record of 76 goals by season's end. Wayne began to speculate about it, too. He made it his objective to beat Esposito's record, with goals against Detroit. Unfortunately, it didn't quite work out that way. Esposito was there, in Detroit, watching the potential record breaker. Nobody had asked Esposito to go, it was just the right thing to do. At the end of the game, Wayne Gretzky had tied — but not broken — Esposito's record. Was he disappointed? Esposito waved off the thought.

"I wanted to be here," he said simply. "I want to be wherever it is he scores his seventy-seventh."

"Wherever" meant Buffalo, where the Oilers would meet the Sabres and where Wayne Gretzky, with 17 games still left in the season, would meet his destiny.

The game was tied 3-3. Winning the game was the team's focus. Number 77 could wait. Somebody — *anybody* — needed to put the puck in the net! Buffalo goalie Don Edwards decided to make Gretzky work for it, stopping four of his shots. Then, the Oilers — and their star player — finally got what they both wanted. The 77th came late in the third period with an elementary wrist shot by Gretzky. With minutes still on the clock, time stood still as the Oilers smothered him. The crowd gave him a standing ovation and Phil Esposito — perhaps remembering the prescient phone call from his father seven years before — personally presented the puck to the man who had beaten his own "personal best."

Oh, and yes, the Oilers also won the game 4-3.

And still it would not end.

There were five games left in the season when the Oilers took to the ice in Calgary. Making an assist on a goal by Pat Hughes, Wayne Gretzky reached another objective: a point total of 200 in one season. Why stop a good thing? Minutes later in the same game, he had another assist, and then, two more goals. At season's end, Wayne Gretzky's final tally was 212 points, 92 goals, and a third Hart Trophy.

Those in the Shadows

Wayne Gretzky made a lot of headlines that season, but he wasn't the only one who helped the Edmonton Oilers climb from fifteenth to second place in the league standings in the space of one season. It took an entire team to do that, young men who played in the shadow of a hockey phenomenon and were proud to do so.

"It doesn't bother me at all," Mark Messier told reporters who asked how he felt about the adulation surrounding Gretzky. "Everybody on this team is going to get their day; it's only a matter of time."

Sporting his big, wide grin, Messier told his teammates, "There's nowhere for us to hide out there, so let's play with reckless abandon!"

In spite of a November ankle injury that bothered him for most of the season, that's exactly what Messier began to do. Others followed his lead. Messier and the other "reckless"

Oilers — Anderson, Coffey, Kurri, and Lowe — were racking up more than a point a game. The end result: 417 goals by the end of the season, something no single team in NHL history had ever achieved. Anderson's point total skyrocketed from 53 to 105. Coffey's bounced from 32 to 89. With 86 points, Kurri, beat his previous season's total by 11.

In the second-to-last game of the 1981-82 season, Gretzky set Messier up for two goals against the L.A. Kings. After the second one, which came less than 30 seconds from the end of the game, Messier did a little dance of glee and there wasn't a face in Northlands Coliseum that wasn't smiling with him. Messier had just scored his 50th goal of the season.

The team made good on Mark Messier's prediction of divisional leadership and came just eight points short of becoming overall league leaders. The team that edged them out was none other than the New York Islanders. It was a portent of things to come.

Soon, it was playoff time. No sweat, the Oilers concluded, given the team they would face in round one. Messier, Coffey, and the others boldly started thinking about who they would meet in round two.

After a first-game loss of 10-8 in round one against the L.A. Kings, the Oilers were incredulous. Wasn't this the lowly fourth-place team in a five-team division? Wasn't this the same team they had beaten seven times in eight games, some by scores as silly as 11-4 and 10-3? This was the L.A. Kings, for pete's sake! Surely game one had to have been an aberration. The score in game two was Oilers 3, Kings 2. That was more like it, but it had been close, with the final Gretzky goal coming in overtime.

Game three in Los Angeles had the standing-room-only crowd in a frenzy. By the end of the second period, things had quieted down substantially as it looked like Grant Fuhr would lead Edmonton to a 5-0 shutout. Early in the third period, the Kings finally managed to squeak one by him, although the L.A. team's owner had already walked out in disgust. Three more L.A. goals soon narrowed the gap, and the crowd suddenly found its voice again. By the end of regulation time, the game was tied and suddenly the Oilers were fighting for a win. Mark Messier gave it his best, but his shot went over the net. In the face-off that followed, the Kings' Doug Smith won the draw. Then, Daryl Evans took the puck and pushed it past Grant Fuhr to give the Kings a 6-5 win.

In game four, it was another close call (3-2) for the Oilers, but a win was a win. There was nothing close about game five, however. It was Kings 7, Oilers 4, in Edmonton, no less. That meant the Kings were off to round two and the Oilers were off the ice until the next season. The *Edmonton Journal* sent the team away for the summer with a terse two-word farewell message: "THEY CHOKED!"

Season of Achievements

The story of the Oilers' 1982-83 season is told well through the achievements of its most valuable players, as well as its statistics. Wayne Gretzky set another record, this one for scoring in consecutive games (the first 30 of the season), which is one reason why he led the league again in scoring with 71 goals and 196 points. Those goals and points were reason enough to give Gretzky his fourth straight Hart Trophy. Messier scored four goals in a single game for the first time in his career and earned a 48-58-106 total, the seventh best in the entire league. The Oilers were divisional leaders (a ridiculous 28 points in front of second-place Calgary) and boasted a new record of 424 goals that placed them just four points behind the league-leading Boston Bruins.

However, none of the Oilers were wearing Stanley Cup rings.

The team was an enormous draw in its hometown, of course, but also, unlike any other team, it had become a huge attraction, playing for 94 percent capacity crowds wherever it landed. Put another way, Wayne, Jari, Mark, and the rest were putting about 1400 more bums in seats at every game than the league average — and contributing about $16,000 extra for the *other* team every time they skated out into someone else's arena.

Behind the Statistics

There were other chapters in the Oilers' tale that turnaround season. Glen Sather was feeling the strain of his multiple roles as general manager, coach, and president. He needed help. The team engine was running full out, but the last playoffs had revealed that it still needed fine-tuning. The team welcomed former defenceman John Muckler as coach. He was the perfect foil for Sather. While Glen was the passionate motivator, Muckler was the cool-headed analyst — exactly what the team needed.

A good year for the team, 1982-83 was, ironically, a lacklustre year for the goalie people had placed so much faith in. In hockey lore, it's called the "sophomore jinx," the second-year slump that many goalies endure. Fuhr's second-season goals against average skyrocketed up to an embarrassing 4.28. By the new year, he was hearing boos from Edmonton fans as he skated on and off the ice after another bad game. Glen Sather and John Muckler agreed on the "tough love" approach that had worked so well with Moog and Messier. Grant was moved down to the Moncton Alpines for 10 games and Andy Moog was out in front of the Oilers' net once again.

Finally, the Finals

The headlines of the venerable *Hockey News* provide a very succinct summary of the three playoff rounds that the Edmonton squad played that year:

"Oilers Waste Little Time Disposing of Winnipeg," was the first headline.

"Oilers Easily Extinguish Calgary's Flames," exclaimed the second.

"Oilers Make It Look Easy Against Hawks," extolled the third.

The Oilers, at last, had gone all the way to the finals. The New York Islanders were waiting.

The season had not been kind to the Islanders. The three-time, Stanley Cup winners were sixth in overall league standings. In the playoffs, however, they had found firm footing and were ready to do battle for the Cup once again. "They" were a squad of seasoned NHL veterans, led, in part, by Mike Bossy, the right-winger who had been the first player in 36 years to score 50-in-50, and the first one to do it in his *rookie* year. It was just the first of four years in which he would achieve the feat. His outstanding performance in the playoffs the year before had earned him the Conn Smythe Trophy. Together with left-winger Clark Gillies and centre Bryan Trottier, "Hawse," as Bossy was known, was ready for another Stanley Cup.

"We wanted that fourth Cup ... to win it by beating Edmonton, already regarded as the NHL's next great team," Bossy wrote later in his autobiography. "We were old and confident, they were young and cocky."

However, it quickly became obvious that Islanders goalie Billy Smith was the man to beat. Smith was a superb playoff netminder, but as excellent as his play was in the finals, it was the "Hatchet Man's" mind games that made the difference. Psychology, not simply physical prowess, allowed the Islanders to beat the Oilers and carry away their fourth

Stanley Cup. That year, the Oilers saw a Billy Smith they had never seen before. Although Smith had been a Dr. Jekyll-like goaltender all season long, the playoffs brought out Mr. Hyde.

Snarling and slashing, Smith challenged the Oilers shooters constantly, leaving the crease, and in spite of his bulky hockey pads, swaggered aggressively into *their* territory. A slash on the leg of Glenn Anderson brought howls of protest from the Oilers' bench. "Suspend him," Sather screamed. Smith just laughed.

Smith coupled a belligerent attitude with outstanding ability. Every time he slapped aside the shots of Lowe, Kurri, Messier, and Gretzky, he slapped aside the team's chances at the Cup. Smith held the high-scoring Edmonton Oilers to only six goals in the entire series. Even the great Gretzky was held scoreless. For his efforts, Smith took home the Conn Smythe Trophy that his teammate, Mike Bossy, had won the year before.

Down with tonsillitis, Bossy saw game one on a TV suspended above his hospital bed. What he saw was a goalie duel between "Smitty" and Andy Moog. Moog was fantastic as he tried desperately to compensate for the lame performance of the Oilers players out in front. However, Smith had all the support he needed (with goals by Duane Sutter and Ken Morrow) to shut Edmonton out 2-0.

"PUBLIC ENEMY NUMBER ONE," shouted the front-page headline in the *Edmonton Journal*. In case there was any confusion, the story was also accompanied by Billy Smith's photograph.

Bossy was on the ice in game two, and surprisingly so was Glenn Anderson.

"Wasn't Anderson hurting?" Billy Smith sneered after the game. "I thought it was his funeral today."

In a way, it was. The Islanders had just buried Anderson and the rest of the Oilers, taking game two 6-3.

Another slash and Wayne Gretzky fell to the ice, another apparent victim of vicious Smith. He was soon back on his skates, shouting and pointing his stick at the goalie. Smith calmly lifted his goal stick to eye level, a few feet from Gretzky's face. The result was a five-minute slashing penalty for Smith. Later, an angry Dave Lumley took revenge and speared Smith in the throat. The best — and worst — was yet to come.

In New York, the Islanders scored four goals in the third period to end a game-three tie and win 5-1. Anxious, it seemed, to enjoy their summer, the Islanders didn't wait long to dominate in game four. Bossy led the scoring with the first of three goals in the first period. While the Oilers struggled to catch up, a frustrated Glenn Anderson skated in front of the net and grazed Smith's mask. Smitty crashed to the ice and lay writhing in front of the goal. The whistle blew and Anderson was out of the game for five long minutes on a high-sticking penalty. Smith struggled to his feet and managed to keep the puck away, giving the Islanders a 4-2 win and the Stanley Cup. It wasn't just the Cup they had won, as the Edmonton Oilers did not need to be reminded, but the Cup in a four-game sweep!

It was a proud and very public moment when Billy Smith accepted the Conn Smythe Trophy at the league's formal presentation. Flashbulbs popped and TV cameras zoomed in. Suddenly, the expected acceptance speech turned into a final, verbal "slash" at the Oilers. There, behind the microphones, Billy admitted that he hadn't really been all that badly hurt in game four — not hurt at all, in fact. He had, he confessed, just faked it.

"I did the same thing to Anderson as Gretzky did to me," he said, without the slightest hint of remorse. "I threw myself on my back on the ice and squirmed around. I want the world and all of Canada to know that two can play at that game."

Chapter 7
The Sweetest Victory

G len Sather was pleased to formally announce what the media gathered before them already knew. The president of the Edmonton Oilers was very proud and pleased to formally introduce five-time Stanley Cup winner, Kevin Lowe. After 18 seasons in the NHL, Lowe was to be the team's new assistant coach.

The newest member of the Oilers coaching staff graciously answered questions. After all the time he had spent with the club, one reporter asked what his most memorable event was. That was easy. Kevin Lowe remembered the day like no other: the day his bright, brash team had battled its way through a repeat Cup series with New York to beat the once-mighty Islanders and take the Stanley Cup home to

Edmonton for the very first time. It was a day unlike any other, a day he knew would probably never come again. Lowe didn't hesitate: "May 19, 1984," he said, overcome with emotion.

A Sobering Season

Although he had left the core of the team intact, Glen Sather had also begun making serious and significant decisions. The first was moving Mark Messier from wing to centre. Messier responded to the challenge and played tougher and harder, like he had never played before. Even a six-day suspension couldn't stop him. Another decision was to trade Tom Roulston to Pittsburgh for centre Kevin McClelland. Pittsburgh had been so unimpressed by McClelland's two goals and four assists after 24 games that they had shipped him off to a farm team. Sather and Fraser were still after potential and they saw it in "Mac." The team also welcomed Grant Fuhr back into the fold.

Other things, such as strategy, did not change. Speed and finesse were the order of the day, as they had been since the Oilers had first become an NHL team. Other teams were watching and learning, too, giving the aggressive offensive line the name "Five Up." Killing penalties was easier when you dedicated two of your best men (Gretzky and Kurri) to the task. Why had nobody else thought to do the same?

The fine 1982-83 season had been, in retrospect, merely a prelude to the one that followed. For most of the last half of the 1983-84 season, while the team was playing and winning, its players were mentally preparing themselves to meet the Islanders. So great was the commitment to beat the Islanders that 28-year-old Lee Fogolin voluntarily turned over his captaincy to Wayne Gretzky. Where there was once youthful, playful banter, there was now purposeful discussion.

They called him "Captain Video." According to Roger Neilson, the former head coach of Toronto, Buffalo, and Vancouver, teams simply couldn't see enough video and film. He had used the medium not only to scout other players, but also to instruct those he had coached, helping them prepare for other teams. Fired the year before by the L.A. Kings (he had the Oilers to thank for that), Neilson had watched Edmonton's humiliation in the finals and thought Glen Sather could use his help. Sather thought so, too. Soon, Neilson went to work, watching, replaying, and then editing tapes of the Islanders into a formidable "best of" collection. It wasn't long before the team began to see results.

Four games into the season, the Oilers were 4-0. Wayne Gretzky thought that maybe the team could average six goals a game throughout the season. They already had two "eights" in those first few games. As the days went by, the Oilers added a "10," an "11," and a "13." In the space of four games, the Oilers kept those high numbers, beating Washington 11-3, Pittsburgh 7-3, Winnipeg 8-5, and Quebec 7-4. After 52 games, the Oilers' average was 5.78 goals per game.

Wayne "Streak" Gretzky couldn't stop scoring. When his scoring hit 40 consecutive games, people started to take notice. The Daoust skate manufacturers had produced a blue and orange skate for the Oilers. Now they were afraid that if Wayne put them on it would end the streak, so they held the skates back. The Titan manufacturers had a new plastic-injected stick. Wayne tested it and loved it. Again, Titan refused to let him use it in games because it might end the streak.

How Sweet It Is

Later that season, the Oilers watched the video and film clips to get ready for their biggest challenge of all. They saw that Billy Smith had trouble behind the net. They made lists of Islanders they knew they would have to prepare for, both mentally and physically. They talked strategy, including how to get players such as Bryan Trottier off his game. They wondered if they could possibly beat the Islanders twice in the first four games, or better yet, in the first two right there in Edmonton.

More than anything, however, they simply wanted to wipe that smirk right off Billy Smith's face. There was no question that it was really Smith who had beaten them. So, Glen Sather played it safe. Grant was in, and, once again, Andy Moog was out. The pressure mounted, but it was toughest on Wayne Gretzky, who had been held scoreless during the last series.

A first-round playoff victory against the Winnipeg Jets was a given. The second round proved to be something else.

The Calgary Flames weren't going to be snuffed out by the Oilers the way they had been in the previous playoffs. Coffey was down with the flu, and Wayne Gretzky was less than great. His parents came to cheer him on, happy to do anything that might work. It took a nasty seven-game series to quench the Flames. By that standard, the last round against Minnesota was a walk in the park, a stroll that led straight to the finals and a rematch with the Islanders.

It had been a lazy, self-satisfied summer and the Islanders had started talking about a "Drive for Five" (five Stanley Cups in a row) to tie the Montreal Canadiens' record. Looking back at it a few months later, Bossy, Trottier, and the others couldn't help feeling disappointed with a season that should have been good enough for them to clinch their division championship again. Expectations were high, but the team's energy was low.

The Oilers' plans were coming to fruition. In a reversal of Smith's first-game shutout in the previous series, Edmonton took the first game 1-0 in Unionville, Long Island. They seemed to be able to anticipate everything the Islanders were going to do. This was Grant Fuhr's show, co-starring newcomer Kevin McClelland, who scored the lone goal in the third period. Preparing for the second game, the Oilers were both relieved and excited. The Islanders were not.

The NHL's schedule change preyed on the minds of the New York players. Already tired, they were frustrated because the usual home game pattern of 2-2-1-1-1 had been altered to save plane fare. Now it was 2-3-2.

"I didn't like that we had to play the middle three games in Edmonton," Mike Bossy remembered. "After falling behind one game to none, I liked it even less."

In game two, Bryan Trottier scored just 53 seconds into the game. Clark Gillies, who had only scored 12 goals all season long, produced a hat trick and the Islanders skated off with a 6-1 win.

And Wayne Gretzky was still scoreless in the series.

In game three, the fans in Northlands Coliseum came alive, and the Oilers responded. In the second period, the Islanders were leading 2-1 until the Oilers scored three goals — the first in a solo dash by Mark Messier, and, with less than one minute remaining, two more just 18 seconds apart by Anderson and Coffey. In the third, Messier scored again and McClelland added one more less than half a minute later.

"Worn out, tired, hurt, and discouraged," Mike Bossy sensed that they were finished. In comparison, the Oilers grew more confident with every period. The 7-2 victory was a costly one, however. Grant Fuhr was caught behind the net and smashed into the boards by two other players. The Oilers' star goalie was taken away with a sprained shoulder. Nonetheless, the Oilers had been practicing those "high numbers" all season long and had gotten to like them, so they repeated the 7-2 score in the fourth game, with Andy Moog in goal to keep the other side of the scoreboard low. At last, The Great One scored, not once, but twice. There was no stopping them now.

Nobody on the team wanted to go all the way back to New York. It was time to put an end to the series, right then and there, in Edmonton. Andy Moog was in goal. The start was ominous, with an Islanders' power play less than a minute into play for the most ridiculous of reasons: too many men on the ice. Kurri and Gretzky, the magic men of Edmonton, provided two goals in the first period and Billy Smith skated slowly away to be replaced with Roland Melanson. The crowd was delighted, screaming, "We want Billeeee!"

Ken Linseman scored on a power play assisted by Gretzky and Charlie Huddy. Within five minutes, on another power play, Jari Kurri scored with assistance from Paul Coffey and Glenn Anderson. Now it was 4-0. The Islanders fought back in the third period, with Pat LaFontaine scoring twice for New York within the first minute. Under great pressure, Moog continued to make excellent saves, until, with 3:15 left, Pat Flatley crashed into the goalie, who lay motionless on the ice. While Flatley went to the penalty box, Moog staggered to his feet. The stunned crowd let out a sigh of relief. With less than 30 seconds of play left, and the New York net wide open, Dave Lumley grabbed the puck on the face-off, and shot it down from the Edmonton end into the open net to make the fifth and final goal.

Fans leapt onto the ice, balloons floated and bounced, and Wayne Gretzky had a tug-of-war with souvenir-hungry fans who wanted his stick. When New York and Edmonton players met each other in two passing lines, in the post-game ritual, the Islanders were doing more than shaking hands. Some of them knew they were passing the Stanley Cup to the next dynasty.

Chapter 8
The Dynasty is Forged

ust before the start of the 1984-85 season, the focus of Canada's hockey fans was not on the NHL, but on the Canada Cup series. There was a lot at stake. Three years earlier, the Soviets had beaten Canada to win the Cup. Glen Sather was the team's new coach and GM and he picked the league's best players for the team, many of whom also played for the Oilers. They included Grant Fuhr, four Oilers defencemen, and three forwards: Anderson, Gretzky, and Messier. Sather's controversial selections provoked a storm of criticism, although the criticism soon melted away as the Oilers and their teammates soundly beat the Soviets and then went on to win the best-of-three finals against Sweden, 5-2 and 6-5. It was a very gratifying way to start the new season.

The Dynasty is Forged

The Oilers continued their winning ways, playing 15 straight games without a loss and celebrating their scoring champs Wayne Gretzky (73 goals) and Jari Kurri (71 goals). Finishing second in the league, the season was also rewarding in other ways. Paul Coffey won his first Norris Trophy and Kurri took away the Lady Byng. Gretzky won the Hart once more, as well as the Art Ross Trophy and the Lester B. Pearson Award.

The "Sather-and-Fraser" team went shopping again. In the fourth-round draft, they chose Esa Tikkanen, a Finnish player destined to have a very exciting start to his NHL career. The team then advanced to what would be a record-setting series of playoffs, setting a total of 25 NHL records, as they beat the L.A. Kings, Winnipeg Jets, and Chicago Blackhawks. They were in the finals again, this time facing the "bad boys" of the 1970s, the Philadelphia Flyers. Ten years later, of course, not many of those "bad boys" were still on the ice. Dave "the Hammer" Schultz, Andre "Moose" Dupont, Reggie Leach, and Bernie Parent were now just memories. Like Glen Sather before him, player-turned-GM Bobby Clarke had been rebuilding the Flyers, with the likes of defenceman Mark Howe, 50-plus-goal-scorer Tim Kerr, new Swedish netminder Pelle Lindburgh, and captain Dave Poulin.

In game one of the Stanley Cup series, Gretzky was scoreless as the Oilers were beaten soundly 4-1. Play was so bad that coaches John Muckler and Glen Sather refused to let the team see the films of the games.

"It's scary how well we're playing," Philadelphia's Mark Howe admitted. "We were just all over them."

What the Flyers needed (and perhaps the Oilers, too), was a little surprise. So, in game two, Wayne Gretzky had a new partner in the line, newcomer Esa Tikkanen. In game two, the Oilers reversed their fortunes, posting a 3-1 win. Back in Edmonton for game three, Gretzky performed magnificently, making seven shots on goal and scoring three in the first period alone to take the game 4-3. Game four began with a sudden onslaught by the Flyers, who leapt into a 3-1 lead before the first period was over. Glenn Anderson tied the game by the end of the second period. In the third, Rick Tocchet dashed from the penalty box straight to the Oilers' goal on a breakaway. Grant Fuhr brushed off his effort, and allowed Wayne Gretzky an opportunity to put the team ahead with two more goals. The final score was 5-3.

The fifth game was almost anticlimactic, with the added attraction of seeing team leaders Glen Sather and Mike Keenan shout back and forth as the Oilers ran away with the game (8-3) and the team's second Stanley Cup.

Another League-Leading Season

The 1985-86 season started well but then went horribly wrong. In an early game with the Flyers, with the score 2-2, Mark Messier was taken out of the face-off circle for jumping the gun (or the puck). When he complained about the call, he was given a two-minute penalty. His absence, and the resulting power play, cost the team the game.

Right after Christmas, the NHL arranged a game with the Russians in Edmonton.

Coming off the Christmas break (replete with turkey and wine), the Oilers were no match for the Soviets. The Oilers lost 5-3 in another high-profile game. Nevertheless, the team wrapped up the season as league leaders with a stunning 56-17-7 record.

We All Make Mistakes
Round one of the playoffs against the Vancouver Canucks was the most lacklustre playoff series the Oilers had experienced in their short NHL history. It was no contest as the Canucks bumbled around on home ice before a crowd that was at less than half its full capacity. Round two, against the Calgary Flames, was a rude slap in the face. So far, the Flames hadn't worried the Oilers. During the season, Edmonton had won five of six games against Calgary and had tied the sixth. Nonetheless, the Flames' sole 9-3 win late in the season had given the Flames an enormous psychological boost going into the playoffs.

Back home in Edmonton for round two of the playoffs, the Oilers were stunned when Calgary beat them soundly once again, 4-1. The Flames, buoyed by the performance of their young goalie, Mike Vernon, grew even more confident. The Oilers managed a 6-5 win in game two but needed overtime to do it. The Flames came back 3-2 in game three.

The Oilers soon stopped the talk about "an upset" by the Flames with a solid 7-4 win in game four. The series was tied, but if the Oilers weren't worried, they should have been. In Edmonton, disbelieving fans watched the Flames singe the Oilers 4-1. Back in Calgary, Flames fans were ready for their team to shut down Edmonton in what they hoped would be the final game. The Oilers felt confident they would be back in Edmonton for game seven. And they were. They extended the series on a 5-2 win.

At the Coliseum for game seven, the game was tied 2-2 after a Flames early 2-0 lead. Then, Edmonton's rookie defenceman, Steve Smith, accidentally banked an errant puck off of Grant Fuhr's leg for a goal on his own net that broke the tie and ended the Oilers' season prematurely. Players on the bench looked up in disbelief.

"What the hell happened?" asked slack-jawed John Muckler. "How is the puck in the net?" Surely there had to be time to get another goal and take the game into overtime. It was not to be.

Peter Pocklington walked over to talk to the tearful player, who was sitting in isolation in the dressing room, but Smith was inconsolable. Nonetheless, the media was waiting and it was time for Steve Smith to take it like a man. It was a dismal and dispiriting end to a season that had held such promise for the team. Now that promise belonged to Calgary, as the Flames prepared for their first Stanley Cup finals.

Up Where They Belong

That summer before the 1986-87 season, the players wondered nervously what changes coach Glen Sather had in mind. There had to be changes after that awful climax to the previous season. Sather did the best thing he could have, at the time, and that was absolutely nothing. All the right talent was in all the right places.

Unfortunately, in Sather's eyes, one "talent"— Paul Coffey — wasn't demonstrating as much as he could have, and the coach said so publicly. However, neither one let their growing animosity hinder the team's fortunes as the season progressed. The embarrassing loss to Calgary focused the players on the task at hand — winning the Cup again. They were soon poised to do so, finishing first in league standings. Gretzky won the scoring championship, while Kurri finished second, and Messier placed fourth. Then, it was time for a Stanley Cup rematch with the Philadelphia Flyers.

It was also time for strategy. The Flyers' rookie goalie, Ron Hextall, was brilliant, but he also had a temper. Fuhr suggested they play rough in the Philly crease, to see if they could ignite that short fuse of his. (This was a legitimate tactic in the last Cup final to be played before the NHL expanded the semicircle crease and years before penalties could be imposed for goalie interference.) In the finals, however, it was the Flyers' goalie who interfered with the Oilers, as Hextall laid out Kent Nilsson with a slash to the back of his legs. Following a series of long, loud calls for his suspension, the league belatedly assessed an eight-game absence against Hextall, although it wouldn't take affect until the *following* season.

The score was tied in the first period of game one. Wayne Gretzky moved the Oilers ahead. A Flyers goal by Brian Propp, late in the second, tied the game again and gave fans an edge-of-their-seat thrill. Then it was Anderson, Coffey, and Kurri, and a 4-2 victory. In game two, another tied score left fans breathless, until Wayne Gretzky put one in the net. Two more Flyers' goals put them ahead in the second period. In the third period, in the face of an overwhelming offensive, Hextall stood firm. The Oilers outshot the Flyers 15-5, but it wasn't until Glenn Anderson snaked his way past the Philly defence that the Oilers registered another goal. Then it was Coffey to Kurri and in the end a 3-2 win for the Oilers.

It looked like three-in-a-row for the Oilers as they led 3-0 early in the second period of the third game. The Flyers rallied and won 5-3. The Oilers took game four handily 4-1 and then lost game five 4-3. Goaltender Ron Hextall kept the Oilers at bay and the Flyers took game six 3-2, forcing a seventh and deciding game. Back in Edmonton, Messier, Kurri, and Anderson made a "come-from-behind" effort to give the Oilers a 3-1 Stanley Cup victory. It was good to be back. Steve Smith got to hold the Cup, after all.

Nonetheless, Hextall's performance had been so fundamental to the Flyers' performance that he was given the Conn Smythe Award as the series MVP.

The "Coffey Break"

After assisting his team to win three Stanley Cup victories in the seven years he had been with the Oilers, defenceman Paul Coffey felt he deserved more respect. The most meaningful way to demonstrate that well-deserved respect, he figured, would be for Sather to tear up his contract and increase his paycheque. Sather refused to do that until the contract was finished.

At the time, Paul Coffey was one of the fastest skaters and highest-scoring defenders in the league. Incurring the displeasure of a player this valuable could have meant a potentially devastating loss. Concerned, perhaps, about setting a dangerous precedent for future negotiations with players, Sather decided to hold his ground. Soon, Peter Pocklington became involved, questioning Coffey's courage. After that, it was difficult for Coffey to come back.

After he missed the first six weeks of the season, Coffey was traded to the last-place Pittsburgh Penguins along with Dave Hunter and Wayne Van Dorp. In return, four players joined the Oilers, including Craig Simpson. The Penguins said they wouldn't negotiate a higher fee with Coffey, but they soon capitulated. Sather shook his head. Paul Coffey was a player, not a team. Negotiations between Glen Sather and Grant Fuhr's agent, Rich Winter, took a tense turn as well. Heated words escalated into a shoving match. However, Fuhr was soon back in the Oilers uniform with a new contract. Mark Messier was also coming back. Andy Moog, however, was a different story.

Discouraged at his lack of ice time since the arrival of Grant Fuhr, Moog took advantage of a new Olympic ruling that allowed professionals to play Olympic hockey. Moog joined the Canadian team during the winter Olympics. Sather then turned to Boston for a trade. The result was an exchange of goalies — Bill Ranford for Andy Moog. Along with Ranford came Geoff Courtnall. At the time, neither team could have guessed how that single trade would affect both their futures at the end of the season.

What started out as a difficult season off the ice also began as a more challenging season in front of the fans. Edmonton's games-won total was down to 44. For the second season in a row, the team posted an under-400-goal total. The Oilers dropped to second place in the Smythe Division behind the Calgary Flames, which became the number one team in the NHL. Out with an eye injury for 16 games, Wayne Gretzky missed out on both the Hart and Ross Trophies for the first time in eight years. Nonetheless, with Lowe, Fuhr, and the new line of Mark Messier (centre), Craig Simpson (left-wing), and Glenn Anderson (right-wing), Edmonton was still a team to be reckoned with.

The Strangest Finals
In round one of the 1987-88 playoffs, reckoning with the Oilers fell first to the Winnipeg Jets. Edmonton ended Winnipeg's Stanley Cup hopes quickly in five games. The result of round

two was even quicker. The Oilers beat the much-touted Flames in just four games. In the third round, the Oilers met the Red Wings. The Red Wings were soon sent packing back to Detroit, smarting from an 8-4 loss in the fifth and deciding game. Meanwhile, the Boston Bruins had battled their way past Buffalo in six games, Montreal in five, and New Jersey in a long seven-game series to win the Wales Conference Championship. Edmonton and Boston, and as it turned out, Grant Fuhr and Andy Moog, would both play for the Stanley Cup.

Bruins coach Terry O'Reilly decided to start Andy Moog in game one. Spirited Oilers defence meant that the Bruins were able to get only 14 shots on Grant Fuhr, one of which lit up the scoreboard. The Oilers did better, winning the game 2-1. The number of shots-on-goal tells the tale of the second game. Edmonton besieged goalie Reggie Lemelin, levelling 32 shots against him, while Boston managed only 12 shots on Grant Fuhr. The Oilers had a 4-2 second-game victory.

One of the most spirited of the Oilers in the series was none other than Steve Smith, who played hard and fast as one of Edmonton's offensive defencemen, clearly outpacing Norris Trophy winner Ray Bourque. The "Flying Finn," Esa Tikkanen, was the hero of game three at the Boston Gardens, scoring a hat trick and contributing mightily to the Oilers 6-3 win.

Then, old age intervened. The aged veteran was not any of the players, but rather, the ancient Boston Gardens, which betrayed its own home team. Boston was playing a tight, hard-fighting contest and was leading 3-2 into the second period. After Craig Simpson put one past former Oilers goalie Andy Moog to tie the score, the lights went out. For a few minutes, there was total darkness. Then, the feeble glimmer of emergency lighting reached the rink surface, but it wasn't enough to complete the game. A combination of heat, humidity, and ancient equipment had brought a hard-fought Stanley Cup game to a standstill. The players and fans filed out.

NHL president John Ziegler met with officials and cited NHL bylaw 27.12c: "If for any cause beyond the control of the clubs, a playoff game should be unfinished, such game shall be replayed in its entirety at the end of the series, if necessary, and it shall be replayed in the rink in which the unfinished game occurred."

Everyone agreed.

When word of the decision reached the Oilers in their dressing room, they were relieved. They could go back to Edmonton and finish the series in style. Besides, nobody was anxious to return to Boston. In that ancient Boston Gardens, who knew what would happen next?

In Northlands Coliseum, the Bruins, with Moog in goal, played bravely in what was called game 4-A, leading 2-1 in the first period. Then, the Flying Finn scored in the second and the Oilers surged ahead. There were just 10 seconds left when Wayne Gretzky passed the puck to Craig Simpson, who angled it in past Andy Moog with a tenth of a second to spare. At the final siren, the score was 6-3 and the Stanley Cup was held high by the Edmonton Oilers, once again.

The Big Trade

In 1988, just weeks after the dynasty had won its fourth Stanley Cup in five years, the NHL held its annual congress in Montreal. Taking a break from the speeches and the planning sessions, Red Fisher, veteran *Montreal Gazette* sports reporter and broadcaster with CBC's *Hockey Night in Canada*, chatted with Vancouver Canucks coach Bob McCammon.

"Have you heard?" McCammon asked. "The Oilers are trying to deal him . . ."

By *him*, of course McCammon meant Wayne Gretzky — The Great One. Fisher hadn't heard. As quickly as he could, however, he buttonholed Edmonton coach John Muckler to ask him if it was true. Muckler said it was nonsense. Then he tracked Glen Sather down in his hotel room. He got virtually the same response.

A couple of days later, over breakfast, Canadiens president Ronald Corey mentioned Gretzky's name. Then the Oilers' marketing people mentioned "a big trade," although Fisher couldn't check it out, because many of them were already gone. Fisher phoned Sather again in Edmonton, who suggested he call Peter Pocklington. During their conversation, the Oilers owner told Fisher that his assumptions were ridiculous. Fisher decided to go on holidays.

Fisher was having a good time in Europe, although he couldn't get the rumours — and the denials — out of his mind. So, more than 9000 kilometres away, he sat down and began typing out a "what if" story.

On July 16, 1988, Wayne Gretzky stood inside Edmonton's St. Joseph's Basilica, the city's biggest church. Wayne was all dressed up, with a black tie and a white corsage. Usher Paul Coffey and everyone else — all 700 guests, in fact — were dressed up. The Great One and his fiancée, Janet, were about to be married. As the hour drew nearer, Paul and Wayne found a moment or two to talk. You could call it "small talk," except for the secret that Wayne soon shared with his former teammate. He confided that Peter Pocklington was trying to trade him.

About three weeks later, in Portugal, Red Fisher's telephone rang. On the other end was Montreal Canadiens sportscaster Dick Irvin.

"There's a press conference about to start in Edmonton," he told Fisher.

Mark Messier was on the golf course when he got the news. He had been phoning Wayne off and on for days, but his friend had not returned his calls. Wayne Gretzky likely knew just how persuasive Messier could be. This time was no exception. As soon as Messier found out about the impending trade, he tried to talk Gretzky out of the move, but to no avail. Next, it was Glen Sather's turn. Sather and Gretzky talked for an hour as the president tried everything he knew to dissuade him. It was no use — Wayne Gretzky's mind was made up. He would soon be on his way to Los Angeles.

Chapter 9
One More Time

vents often converge. In popular sports' history, the decline of the Edmonton Oilers began when a financially beleaguered owner decided to trade away his biggest asset to help counteract losses in his other businesses.

However, even before the trade was formulated, other seemingly unrelated challenges were threatening the team — the loss of a tremendous talent such as Wayne Gretzky was just the most public. Less public was the challenge of finding the new talent needed to continually renew the team's youth and vitality. Scouting prowess, once the domain of a select few, such as Barry Fraser, was now more commonplace. There were great players out there, but Edmonton wasn't getting them.

In the years following Esa Tikkanen's selection in 1983, luck and timing, those largely uncontrollable factors, had made the right picks an elusive thing for the Oilers. Many of the players selected in the drafts had played so fleetingly with the Oilers that they were soon forgotten. Some never played at all. It was little wonder that Peter Pocklington got fed up and bypassed Glen Sather altogether to enter into negotiations directly with Tikkanen. Sather preferred a more leisurely approach, which didn't suit Pocklington. Shaken by the almost-overwhelming negative reaction to the Gretzky trade, he simply wanted the new deal with Tikkanen to be concluded quickly.

Playing Past the Pain

Perhaps Glenn Anderson said it best. Starting the 1988-89 season without Wayne Gretzky, he said, was like mourning the death of a brother.

While clearly devastated, Mark Messier, now the captain of the team, attempted to rally the players, urging the team to get going and move forward into the new season. That was easier said than done. Yet, it had to be done, and early in the season it looked as if the Edmonton Oilers were going to do it. First they beat the Islanders, then trounced Winnipeg with a winning goal by Kevin Lowe. Then it was time to meet the Kings. In the pre-game skate, the Northlands' crowd gave their lost hockey hero a standing ovation and began chanting his name. It was a modest beginning for Gretzky — the Kings lost 8-6, and he assisted in just two of the six goals — but Messier scored twice against his friend's new team.

Messier's six-game suspension just a few days later, in the wake of a particularly punishing blow to Canucks player Rich Sutter, didn't help team morale, or performance. "Inadvertent," was the league's verdict, but the suspension was not revoked.

By mid-October, Glen Sather admitted that his team's performance had been less than stellar. It got worse. At the end of the season, Edmonton's record of 38-34-8 put them in third place in the Smythe Division. There was still a lot of power on the team, with high-scoring aces Jari Kurri, new-comer Jimmy Carson (received in the Gretzky trade), and, of course, Mark Messier. It was enough to send the Oilers to the playoffs once again. Their first round opponents: the L.A. Kings and Wayne Gretzky.

Inside Inglewood's Fabulous Forum, Mark Messier per-formed well in the series opener, with a goal and two assists, to lead his team to a 4-3 win. The Kings evened the series 1-1 the next night with a 5-2 victory, in which Gretzky scored one goal. Back in Edmonton for game three, many of the same fans who had stood and applauded The Great One at the start of the season now booed him in reaction to his complaints in the media about Glen Sather. Messier crunched Gretzky into the boards.

"The first thing that went through my mind? That Janet wouldn't like it," Messier laughed later.

The Oilers won, 4-0.

Kevin Lowe gave the team its winning goal in game four, smacking Messier's rebounded puck back into the net with less than half a minute left to play. The game was 4-3; the series was 3-1. In Los Angeles, Gretzky provided three points for a 4-2 Kings win and then L.A. won another in Edmonton, 4-1. Game seven in the Forum was a tense contest. It was tied up 3-3 halfway through and then it became the L.A. Kings' show. The final score was 6-3, a stunning triumph for Gretzky and his new team, and a demoralizing defeat for past friends and teammates.

Champions Again

The Edmonton Oilers had a lot to prove in the 1989-90 season, especially after the disappointing previous year. Peter Pocklington's cash-strapped ways meant that putting together a Cup-winning team was becoming more and more difficult. Many of the team's former Stanley Cup winners were now playing against the Oilers, instead of with them.

Had Wayne Gretzky's departure meant that much to the club's winning ways?

It hadn't, not according to Mark Messier, his heir apparent, or to Glen Sather, whose deftness in drafts and deals was still bringing new players on board, including young up-and-at-'em players such as Adam Graves and Joe Murphy. With these two new additions and Martin Gelinas, the Oilers had a line that had started to produce.

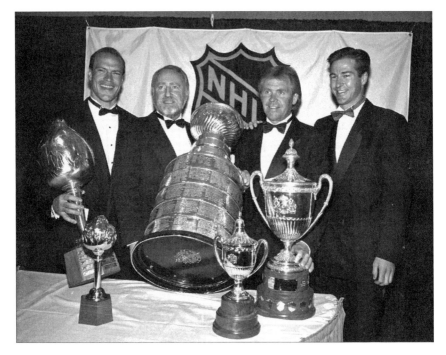

Left to right: Mark Messier, Peter Pocklington,
Glen Sather, and Kevin Lowe at the 1990 NHL Awards

The number one power line of Mark Messier, Jari Kurri,
and Esa Tikkanen was still devastatingly effective. When
injuries sidelined Grant Fuhr late in the season, Bill Ranford
was ready to take over in the crease. There was young blood,
too. Adam Graves was a bright, fast addition to the team, and
he scored often. Messier was more focused and energetic,
clearly the leader Glen Sather needed him to be. The past
was, well, the past. The present was fleeting. It was the future

that Messier was focused on as he pulled his team toward his vision of another Stanley Cup victory.

Messier was still an excellent player. The 1989-90 season was his best yet: hat tricks on three different occasions added up to multiple points in 41 of the team's 79 regular-season games. At the end of it all, Mark Messier's 45-84-129 goal-assist-point record was a mere 13 points shy of Wayne Gretzky's own set of statistics. The Oilers finished second in their division that year, just nine points behind Calgary, fifth in the league, and better than the year before.

The playoffs went, well, the way Oilers' playoffs were meant to go. In round one, the Winnipeg Jets made the Oilers work for their series' victory. Behind three games to one, Messier marshalled the troops and Edmonton took the next three games. Next, it was time to dethrone the Kings. Oh, but how the mighty fall! The score in the first game was Oilers 7, Kings 0. In the second it was Oilers 6, Kings 1. Could it be this easy? In Los Angeles, the Edmonton squad rolled up two more wins, 5-4 and 6-5 in overtime. Six games later, the Oilers had beaten the Blackhawks and were soon playing for the Cup once again, against the Boston Bruins.

The first game against the Bruins was so long, it was as if the crowd had paid to see what baseball fans called a "twilight double-header." Close to an hour into overtime, most of the Edmonton first-stringers (and most of the Bruins) were clearly exhausted. Glen Sather decided to take Petr Klima off the bench and put him on the ice.

When Detroit had traded Klima for Jimmy Carson, the Red Wings had wished the Oilers luck with a player they considered to be lazy. However, as soon as Messier put him on the line between himself and Anderson, Klima suddenly found the inspiration he needed. That night, he made a powerful contribution, managing to score on former Oilers goalie Andy Moog to finish the longest game in Stanley Cup history.

The other games were shorter, but no less sweet, thanks in no small measure to goalie Bill Ranford, who, at the end of this momentous series would cradle the Conn Smythe Trophy. The second game ended with a resounding 7-2 win for the Oilers. Boston took game three 2-1 in Edmonton, and then the Oilers were back, with a pair of 5-1 and 4-1 victories.

Holding the Cup high, Messier slowly skated over to his parents, to share the moment with them. It had been a long journey from that frozen pond by the highway in Portland, Oregon. *Hockey News* was there, and the camera shutter clicked. The happy victory photo ran on the paper's cover, accompanied by a one-word headline: "REDEMPTION."

Of Men and Money
The next season started without Jari Kurri. Contract negotiations had not gone well. For a while, protracted negotiations with Glenn Anderson had many also doubting his eventual return.

However, there was another absence that was more

The Edmonton Oilers win the 1990 Stanley Cup.
Left to right: Kevin Lowe, Mark Messier, and Jari Kurri

keenly felt by the team. Grant Fuhr, who never seemed to lose his cool, had a problem. After successfully completing treatment, the star goalie was suspended for 60 games for cocaine use.

He just wanted to be a "normal guy," he later told *Edmonton Journal* reporter Dan Barnes. However, he wasn't "normal." He was Grant Fuhr, a trophy-winning goalie for the Edmonton Oilers. Looking for escape, Fuhr had found drugs.

"I led a double life," the future Hall-of-Famer explained. It was just one of many problems that now plagued the team.

As the first years of Pocklington's financially constrained decade ground away at the once-mighty Oilers, it's not likely that either Peter Pocklington or Glen Sather saw the 1990-91 season as a new beginning. They might just as easily have felt it was the beginning of the end, as it had been with the collapse of WHA. However, unlike those earlier, happier days, there were now clouds on the Edmonton Oilers' hockey horizon.

By the mid-1990s, Glen Sather's champagne-and-caviar days were done. Nonetheless, the coach continued to soldier on resolutely into the new millennium, facing diminishing budgets and spiralling player costs.

Pocklington redoubled his efforts to unload the team. "Sold," announced the headline in the *Edmonton Journal* in March of 1997. Fans were fearful: would the team leave town? A year later, however, a group of Edmonton investors fashioned a solid financial solution that would keep the Oilers in Edmonton, where they belonged.

Bibliography

Allen, Kevin and Bob Duff. *Without Fear.* Chicago, Illinois: Triumph Books, 2002.

Bossy, Mike. *Boss.* Toronto, Ontario: McGraw-Hill Ryerson, 1988.

Carpiniello, Rick. *Messier: Steel on Ice.* Toronto, Ont. Stoddart, 1999.

Dowbiggin, Bruce. *Of Ice and Men.* Toronto, Ontario: Macfarlane Walter & Ross, 1998.

Fisher, Red. *Hockey, Heroes and Me.* Toronto, Ontario: McClelland and Stewart, 1994.

Fischler, Stan. *Golden Ice: The Greatest Teams in Hockey History.* Scarborough, Ont., McGraw-Hill Ryerson Ltd., 1990.

Falla, Jack, editor. *Quest for the Cup 1917-2000.* Toronto, Ontario, Key Porter, 2001.

Frayne, Trent et al. *Hockey Chronicles: An Insider History of National Hockey League Teams.* Toronto, Ontario: Key Porter Books, 2000.

Greenberg, Jay. *The Full Spectrum.* Toronto, Ontario: Dan Diamond and Associates, 1996.

Gretzky, Walter and Jim Taylor. *Gretzky.* Toronto, Ont., McClelland and Stewart, 1984.

Gretzky, Wayne and Rick Reilly. *An Autobiography.* New York: HarperCollins, 1990.

Gzowski, Peter. *The Game of Our Lives.* Toronto, Ontario: McClelland and Stewart, 1981.

Hesketh, Bob and Francis Swyripa, editors. *Edmonton: The Life of a City.* Edmonton, Alberta: NeWest Publishers Ltd., 1995.

Hunter, Douglas. *A Breed Apart: An Illustrated History of Goaltending.* Chicago, Illinois: Triumph Books, 1995.

Champions: The Illustrated History of Hockey's Greatest Dynasties. Toronto, Ontario: The Penguin Group, Penguin Books Canada Ltd., 1997.

The Glory Barons. Toronto, Ontario: Viking, 1999.

Jenish, D'Arcy. *The Stanley Cup: A Hundred Years of Hockey at Its Best*. Toronto, Ontario: McClelland and Stewart Inc., 1992.

Jones, Terry. *The Great Gretzky Yearbook II*. Toronto, Ontario: General Paperbacks, 1982.

Klein, Jeff. *Messier*. Toronto, Ontario: Doubleday Canada, 2003

Lowe, Kevin, Shirley Fischler, and Stan Fischler. *Champions*. Scarborough, Ontario: Prentice-Hall Canada, Inc., 1988.

McFarlane, Brian. *One Hundred Years of Hockey*. Toronto, Ontario: Deneau Publishers, 1989.

Strachan, Al, editor. *One Hundred Years of Hockey*. Toronto, Ontario: Key Porter Books, 1999.

Weir, Glenn et al. *Ultimate Hockey*. Toronto, Ontario: Stoddart, 1999.

Acknowledgments

The Edmonton Oilers' dynasty ran from 1984 to 1990. In the 15 years since Mark Messier led the team to its last Stanley Cup victory, no other team has come close to equalling its record. There are many who doubt any other NHL team ever will. Ironically, that fatalistic prediction has little to do with the ability of players. It has more to do with the ability of team owners to buy talent. Free agency minimizes the chances that team backers will be able to afford — and therefore, keep — the talent a team already has in place.

The evidence continues to mount. In the 1990s, only two teams managed more than a single Stanley Cup victory. Once in a while, there is a brief flare of hope that a modestly financed franchise can somehow — with luck, timing, and determination — break free of its financial limitations and go all the way. Edmonton hockey fans don't have to look too far over the horizon for proof of this possibility. Why, look at those former rivals, the Calgary Flames!

Such dominance by a single hockey team — a "dynasty" — has only rarely been achieved by a handful of teams, usually in a six-team league. However, the Oilers' rise occurred in a league of over 20 teams. Moreover, the feats of the Edmonton Oilers, and those of many of its individual players, are among the most astonishing in NHL history. It's surprising then that only a few books have ever been published about the Edmonton Oilers — a paltry selection when you consider that, for most of one entire decade, this particular team almost single-handedly defined professional hockey excellence.

Of that handful of books, fewer still tell the entire story. Most, including the engaging *Gretzky* by The Great One's father Walter Gretzky, end just as the team's Stanley Cup ascendancy began.

There are many books that relate the life and times of outstanding individual Oilers' team members (including two about Mark Messier, one about Dave Semenko, and many more about Wayne Gretzky). This may be one reason why the entire story of the *team* has never been told in a popular way. As Wayne Gretzky's phenomenal feats overshadowed those of his teammates so, too, have they dominated the bookshelves. Books about Gretzky, Messier, and others appear to tell the team's story. However, these are player histories, not Oilers histories.

Early in 1980, renowned and respected broadcaster and writer Peter Gzowski knew *something* was happening out in Edmonton. Wayne Gretzky, who Gzowski had met and interviewed some years before, encouraged him to come out west and see for himself. The result was a book called *The Game of Our Lives*, an elegant, game-by-game description of a single season for a team that, even then, seemed destined for greatness.

Champions is an autobiography of defenceman Kevin Lowe. It is a meticulously accurate historical record written by veteran hockey researchers/writers Stan and Shirley Fischler. Unfortunately, Lowe's first-person reminiscences, which do not begin until Chapter 13, end in 1988, somewhat prematurely as it turned out.

To learn more about the later years of the Oilers, one must turn to *The Glory Barons*, by one of the sport's notable chroniclers, Douglas Hunter. This excellent book places much of its focus on the "political and economic issues" that helped to create the team and then bring it to its knees.

All of these works, and others, were extremely valuable to me in my efforts to tell the story of the final dynasty.

Photo Credits

About the Author

BC-born author Rich Mole has enjoyed an eclectic communications career, as a former broadcaster, a freelance journalist, and, for 20 years, the president of a successful Vancouver Island advertising agency. A lifelong fascination with history has fuelled his desire to write about the times and people of Canada's past. Rich now makes his home in Calgary, Alberta.

AMAZING STORIES
by the same author

AMAZING STORIES™

GREAT STANLEY CUP VICTORIES

Glorious Moments in Hockey

HOCKEY

by Rich Mole

ISBN 1-55153-797-4

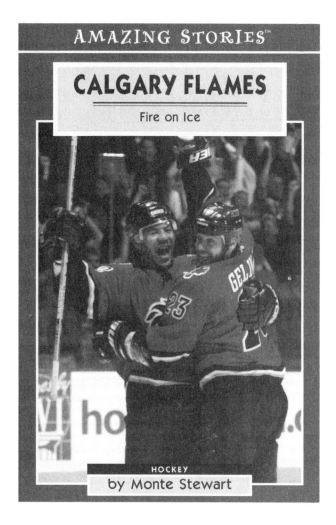

AMAZING STORIES™

CALGARY FLAMES

Fire on Ice

HOCKEY
by Monte Stewart

ISBN 1-55153-794-X

AMAZING STORIES™

OTTAWA SENATORS

Great Stories From The
NHL's First Dynasty

HOCKEY

by Chris Robinson

ISBN 1-55153-790-7

OTHER AMAZING STORIES

These titles are available wherever you buy books. If you have trouble finding the book you want, call the Altitude order desk at 1-800-957-6888, e-mail your request to: orderdesk@altitudepublishing.com or visit our Web site at www.amazingstories.ca

New AMAZING STORIES titles are published every month.